What people are saying abou

Donna fearlessly invites you into her life and ministry. At first you might find yourself nervous about entering this private space, for it is an invitation into a place that might feel unusual, even a wee bit crazy. Occasionally it is downright hilarious. Often it is touching and profoundly moving. She offers you the gift of unprejudicial love for others and unabashed love for Jesus. Her stream-of-consciousness approach to sharing her heart and her gifts of insight on ministry will take you along with her as though you were travelling down a river with her on a raft. It is a journey worth taking. Her perspectives on life and ministry are unique, disarming, heartwarming, challenging, and provocative. Her candid but loving perspective on the people in her unpredictable world of ministry is refreshing. The utter simplicity of her faith in God is stunning.

Wendy J. Porter, PhD,
Director of Music and Worship
McMaster Divinity College

Donna's book *Confessions of an Unlikely Pastor's Wife* is filled with honest, heartfelt, and humorous stories of the struggles and rewards of pursuing the heart of God, as a mother and a pastor's wife, in the midst of the impossibility of ministry life.

Jason Hildebrand
Actor, Creative Catalyst

Confessions of an Unlikely Pastor's Wife is gut-wrenchingly true, as I can attest to many of the stories I have heard and experienced over the twenty years that I have known Donna. My first introduction to Donna was twenty years ago when I received a phone call from her asking about the moms' group, MOPS, that we were holding at a Baptist Church. I had been praying that God would bring Christian moms to our group, as we had so many community moms, we needed additional leaders who would live out their faith among the women. What an amazing answer to prayer! Donna lives her life with integrity, candour, and authenticity, both in reality and amazingly as told in the pages of this book.

The book is laced with humour, which God has gifted Donna with. Together we have belly-laughed and cried over the years. We have served side by side, and it has been my honour and privilege to witness many of the mighty acts of God that Donna shares with her readers. This book is less about Donna and so much more about God. Thank you, Donna, for giving God the glory throughout your life.

Melodie Bissell
CEO and President
Plan to Protect®

CONFESSIONS
of an
Unlikely
Pastor's Wife

Donna Lea Dyck

CONFESSIONS OF AN UNLIKELY PASTOR'S WIFE
Copyright © 2015 by Donna Lea Dyck

All rights reserved. Neither this publication nor any part of this publication may be reproduced or transmitted in any form or by any means, electronic or mechanical, including photocopying, recording or any information storage and retrieval system, without permission in writing from the author.

Unless otherwise indicated, all Scripture quotations are from The Holy Bible, English Standard Version® (ESV®), copyright © 2001 by Crossway, a publishing ministry of Good News Publishers. Used by permission. All rights reserved. Scripture quotations marked NIV are taken from the Holy Bible, NEW INTERNATIONAL VERSION®. Copyright © 1973, 1978, 1984, 2011 by Biblica, Inc. All rights reserved worldwide. Used by permission. NEW INTERNATIONAL VERSION® and NIV® are registered trademarks of Biblica, Inc. Use of either trademark for the offering of goods or services requires the prior written consent of Biblica US, Inc.

Names may have been changed to protect individuals' identities.

Printed in Canada

ISBN: 978-1-4866-0978-9

Word Alive Press
131 Cordite Road, Winnipeg, MB R3W 1S1
www.wordalivepress.ca

MIX
Paper from
responsible sources
FSC® C016245

Library and Archives Canada Cataloguing in Publication

Dyck, Donna Lea, 1960-, author
        Confessions of an unlikely pastor's wife / Donna Lea
Dyck.

Issued in print and electronic formats.
ISBN 978-1-4866-0978-9 (paperback).--ISBN 978-1-4866-0979-6
(pdf).--ISBN 978-1-4866-0980-2 (html).--ISBN 978-1-4866-0981-9
(epub)

        1. Dyck, Donna Lea, 1960-. 2. Church work--Ontario--Toronto.
3. Spouses of clergy--Ontario--Toronto--Biography. I. Title.

BV4404.C3D93 2015   253.092   C2015-903135-4
                                            C2015-903136-2

*This book is dedicated to my husband, Bill,
and my four beautiful adult children,
Lisa, Martin, Andrew and Michael.*

*Each one has walked this journey with me;
I thank God for every step.*

Contents

Acknowledgement

A special thank you to Julie Kraulis for the beautiful cover art.

Dear Reader

This is not a long book; it should be a quick read, so go get a cup of tea and make yourself comfortable in your favourite chair. I would like to tell you what I have seen God do and the lessons I have learned in ministry.

Perhaps you are considering a life of ministry, but feel small and not up to the task. I am praying for you as you read. May the Lord Himself encourage you and whisper in your ear.

If you are a fellow Pastor's wife reading this, I am praying for you also. I know your journey is very different them mine, but you will recognize some stories, as they are likely not far off from some of your own. To you my sister, I would like to say, God sees you in your service for Him. There is not one sacrifice or hardship that is unseen by Him. I pray that your heart will be inspired as you read.

To those of you who know me and were kind enough to simply want to read this: may your faith grow and may you be inspired to believe God for even greater things ahead in your own life and ministry.

I could have written a longer book, but this is what I believe God has given to me. I do not want to go beyond that. May He bless each of you as you read.

Sincerely,
Donna Lea Dyck

So even to old age and gray hairs, O God do not forsake me, until I proclaim your might to another generation.

Psalm 71:18

Confessions of an Unlikely Pastor's Wife

I

KITTENS ARE ONE OF MY FAVOURITE ANIMALS IN ALL GOD'S CREATION. I find life in the country lonely at times. So I've been praying for a kitten. My husband was raised on a hog farm, where kittens and cats belonged in the barn. Not in my world! These creatures were my best friends growing up. Today God answered my heartfelt prayer. As I was driving, I saw a tiny calico kitten sitting on the side of the road. I thought for sure I was doing what Jesus would do—I rescued it from certain death. I've named it "Kitten"—a creative name, I know.

Bill was less than impressed when he came home. He said he was all for Jesus taking the kitten home—His home. Bill made his point, then I made mine, and won. He'll get used to her. Hopefully she'll have kittens herself one day. It's a good thing Bill can't read my thoughts!

When we were in Bible college we knew we wanted to spend our lives in ministry. Since then, we've been involved in an outreach ministry with Youth Unlimited. This suits me perfectly. Yet I know there's a problem. Bill is better suited to be a pastor than a Youth Unlimited worker.

Honestly, that idea scares me. I'm an odd choice for a pastor's wife. Shouldn't a pastor marry a woman who was raised by missionaries or ministers? That sure is not my story. I had an amazing mom, who taught me a lot about life, but she didn't get along very well with Jesus and was even less impressed with ministers and the church.

My dad has been gone for a while. In his last years, he was more sober than we had ever seen him. I'm very thankful for that. He was an alcoholic, and my parents fought a lot. I came out of that with a lot of hurt. I'm very thankful that Jesus is the healer of broken hearts! He's been working in my heart for a long time now. Learning to let go of the past and forgive my dad has made a huge difference in me.

The pastors' wives I know are kind, gentle, and soft-spoken. I know very well that I speak my mind a little too quickly. I like to read spy stories and murder mysteries along with books that inspire me. I struggle with anxiety and always have. I can be gracious and diplomatic, but I'm not always. I'm a work in progress. I'm very thankful for God's patience with me.

When I think about it, I realize that the pastors' wives I've met were all different. That's the good news. They were very godly—weren't they? I don't consider myself super godly. If that's a requirement, we're in trouble.

Furthermore, pastors don't really have weekends off, do they? That thought does not thrill me at all. I love our weekends.

When I gave my life to Jesus, I didn't set up a rulebook for Him with a strict list of career choices for Bill or myself. Bill being a pastor was not something I really considered…like, ever! But, I choose to trust Him with all the details. Even the details I don't know about yet!

When the phone rang today, I was shocked to hear it was an elder from a church in northern British Columbia, asking if Bill would consider a youth-and-worship pastoral position. I feel like maybe God is in a bit of a rush to answer this inquiry of ours. I was just beginning to get used to the possibility of being a pastor's wife!

I'm confident that it would suit Bill perfectly. Two things I know: he's musically gifted, and he loves young people.

I can't say living in a northern climate is a dream come true, considering that I think I have an allergy to the cold!

We're going to "candidate." That's like a tryout for pastors. I've never heard of it before. As long as they don't ask me to sing or play the piano, I'll be fine.

I thought that cities were crazy dangerous at times but not small towns. Last night I woke up when I heard a noise in the kitchen. I was sure it wasn't the dog. I tried to wake up Bill, but he was in a deep sleep. I put my bathrobe on and then crept quietly to my kitchen. There, sitting at the kitchen table, was one of our neighbours, drunk out of his mind!

I tried to act casual, offering to make tea. He said he wanted the name and address of the Anglican minister who lives in our town. I asked him why, and he said he was planning to go over and kill him. I told him that I would go get Bill and they could talk about it. My heart was pounding pretty hard. I went to wake up my husband, my protector.

Bill, who is a pretty mild-mannered man, went very quickly to the kitchen and leaned down into this man's face and told him he was not welcome to walk into our home at two in the morning and ask such foolish questions. Bill got dressed and then walked the guy home. He warned him that if he hears that the Anglican minister is hurt at all, he'll call the police and give them his name.

What a crazy night! It made me wonder what exactly being a pastor is like. You'd think it would be a pretty safe profession! That Anglican minister will never know that there was a guy in our small town wanting to kill him. Even here, life is never dull! I think we might have to lock our doors at night. Most people in this town don't bother. That might change...at least for us!

I know that Jesus watches over our lives. I can trust Him to keep us safe in His hands no matter what. He knows the day He has planned to call us to heaven, and no one can alter His timing.

Jeremiah 29:11 says that God knows the plans He has for us—to give us a future and a hope. I choose to believe Jesus, today and every day.

Last year, Bill and I took in a fifteen-year-old for a few months. He was from a Christian home but was not getting along with his parents at all. It had been a year since we'd seen or heard from him.

Last week I had a bizarre experience—a dream, perhaps. I was fast asleep but was awakened. I felt like I had claws pressed into my arm. A demon was boasting to me. He said, "We have Dan; you have lost him." I woke Bill up and told him what happened. We climbed out of bed, got on our knees, and began to pray for this young man.

Two days later, the phone rang in Bill's office. It was this very same young man. He was calling to tell Bill about something amazing that had happened to him. He had tried to take his life two nights earlier but was unsuccessful. The doctor said it's a miracle that he's still here. "I should be dead," he said.

Bill told this young man that we had been praying for him that very night. He became very quiet on the phone when he heard that. Bill told him again to put his trust in God and prayed with him. I love how God reaches down into the terrible places people find themselves and rescues them. It's weird that the enemy would come and boast to me. He didn't expect that God would step in and save the young man's life.

I wonder how mothering looks as a pastor's wife. Do people look at you as the example of amazing motherhood? I have two beautiful kids, Lisa and Martin. Each is a precious gift in his or her own way. How in the world am I going to get Lisa to sit still? She's three years old and never stops moving. This year in the Christmas pageant, they made her a bumblebee, because she could move wherever and whenever. I don't think tying her to a pew would go unnoticed!

I'm glad I can bake and cook now. Poor Bill must have been tired of all the spaghetti and Hamburger Helper. Cookbooks saved the day! I know pastors' wives do a lot of entertaining, at least a few I know do. I take seriously that verse that tells me to be anxious for nothing but to pray and Jesus will help me. I've even prayed over gravy, and it turned out amazing. I give God full credit!

The Word tells me in 1 Corinthians 1:7, "You are not lacking in any gift." I'm thankful I can rest in what His Word says. I'll need all the help I can get as a pastor's wife.

I'm also worried about how perfect my house will need to be at every moment of every day. That's scary to think about it. I practice something called "company cleaning." When company is coming, I clean. I try not to be too messy, but I'm a long way from the perfect housekeeper! I clean like a mad woman when I know people are coming over.

Bill was worried about my sanity today. When he walked in the door after work, he saw me lying on the floor. On the other side of the Scrabble board was my cat and all her kittens, lying in a row. We were playing Scrabble—I think they were winning! I was just bored. He had to work late, the kids were sleeping, I wanted to play Scrabble, and the only breathing things nearby were the cat and her kittens. Anyway, I think he was joking, though he did seem a bit worried.

We got the date today for when we're going to candidate at that church. We've never been there before. In fact, I've never heard of this place. To say I'm nervous would be putting it lightly. I think I've made my fears pretty clear. If it all works out and we do move, I'll miss our wonderful friends we've made here. I know the name of almost every person in this town, not to mention their dogs and cats. When my mother came to visit, they put it in the local paper!

I know God is leading us. I'm praying for peace in both our hearts and for the congregation about to meet us.

We have to take two planes to get to this northern city. It's a long way from Toronto, where I grew up, and the prairie town I'm now familiar with. Apparently moose and bears have been known to wander into town. That's crazy!

Bill seems pretty nervous, but he's going to do great. He doesn't love public speaking. Good thing he just has to lead the worship music and meet people. He's excellent at both of those activities. We really need the Holy Spirit to lead us.

I'm curious about the houses there. If we do end up there, I'm praying for a nice kitchen. I like kitchens!

The people here are so nice. They love laughing—that's very clear. It's a pretty big church—about 400 people. Bill seems to be the exact opposite of the senior pastor in almost every way. I guess that's a good thing.

The country up here is beautiful, and the air is so clean! I saw one house I especially liked. It had a big bright kitchen—wow! I would love to have a kitchen like that!

Tonight the elders meet to talk to Bill and ask him whatever they feel they need to know. I trust that God will give Bill peace. I know he has his own set of fears that are very different from my own.

I think Lisa and Martin would have a lot of fun here. There are lots of young families.

I know we would have a great time with these people. They seem to have hearts that really want to know and experience God in a deeper way.

The flight back was great. We have a resting peace about moving up north if they should call us back. It's strange, though—the people didn't seem to have any special expectations of me. They didn't even ask me if I play piano or sing. That's always a good sign in my books. So, now we wait. They said they will phone us over the next few days.

I'm thankful that it's the Lord who leads His people. I love how He describes the way He leads in Psalm 23. I know people often see this as a psalm of comfort for those suffering loss or death. Yet, only one verse in the whole psalm mentions suffering or death. To me, it's more a psalm for the living. I love how He leads me and restores me to do whatever He calls me to do. I love His constant presence, because it's a great comfort to me. There's nowhere we can go where He is not with us; His presence is all around.

It seems that many of us have to sit in God's waiting room, wondering what's next. Sometimes He acts promptly, which is certainly my preference. I do know that even in the waiting room He has lessons for us. I really hope I catch on to them! It's not my favourite place to hang out. Yet it seems that everyone has to spend a little time there! I need God to help me be good at waiting.

I know I worry way too much. This is a habit I developed over many years. I need God's help to conquer it. There's also my habit of speaking my mind. My list of things to improve on is growing.

I told Bill that I'm worried about being a pastor's wife because I'm not the silent type. I think that would be a good trait for a pastor's wife. She could embarrass her husband if she said the wrong thing in the wrong setting. Don't people watch the pastor's wife all the time? I guess they would be watching the pastor too. When he blows it or does something stupid, everyone finds out. In fact, I doubt that they hear the real version of the story! That's alarming to think about. Clearly, I need to reread Psalm 23!

The phone rang first thing this morning. It was a unanimous decision, they said. The elders board wants us to come. We start there in one month. Bill didn't mention to them how long it will take to sell a house in this small town. I just want to point out that the last house that sold took two years! Not many people are dreaming about living here. We need God to step in and do what seems impossible.

Bill said he'll call the realtor. I'm going to have to keep the house company-clean all the time. I hope I don't have a nervous breakdown! It's not easy to keep a house company-clean all the time when you live with two small children. Their toys are always ending up everywhere!

If God wants us in the north at that church, we'll need a house to live in. That requires money, all of which is tied up in *this* house. Jesus has three weeks to sell it. We have to trust God in this. It's not like this is a stunning house. It's nice, but far from perfect. My job now is to keep the house clean, company-clean, and His job is to sell it!

It's been three weeks now. Not one person has even walked through our house! The neighbours think we're crazy. They reminded us yet again that the last house to sell in this town took two years. As if I could forget! I know God is up for the task. I just have to go and look at the well next to my house to be reminded.

Two years ago, when the old well ran dry, Bill had to dig a new well by hand. People in this town pay a lot of money to dig down eighty feet, because that's the water level here. Digging that well would cost far beyond anything Bill and I could afford. Actually, we had nothing. We make enough to pay the mortgage and buy groceries and not much else beyond that.

When the townspeople heard that Bill was digging a well by hand, they thought he was nuts. They would drop by to watch. An elder from the church did that water-witching thing with a willow branch. Then he said to Bill, "Dig here." I saw Bill mark the spot, and then he stood in front of it and prayed. I know that God heard that prayer. Our pastor came to help dig. They hit water at twelve feet! They dug a bit more to be sure that the water flow was strong.

Then we called a company that provides well cribbing. We explained to the man on the phone that we didn't have any money at the moment but would pay him once our income tax rebate arrived. He said, "No, this is a gift." The cribbing was provided, and then someone else sent a tractor to dig the trench to run the water line that connects the new well to the house—also without charging us. Since the day that well was dug two years ago, we've never run out of water.

If God can help us hit water at twelve feet instead of eighty, then I'm confident that He's big enough to sell this house. If He wants us to go and pastor at that northern church, He has to sell the house!

My friend phoned this morning. She may know someone who is interested in our house! She's bringing them over to see it. I can't make the house any more company-clean than it already is. We're down to the wire. "God, please sell this house!"

Sold! They loved the house, and we got our asking price! Thank You, Jesus! He does all things well. Now I need to become an expert packer. I've never packed up a whole house in my life!

God's ways and means really are not ours. It's not uncommon that we will find ourselves with no other option than simply trusting Jesus. He taught us to pray "Give us this day our daily bread" (Matthew 6:11). He said, "Apart from me you can do nothing" (John 15:5). We're in fact dependent upon Him. This also means that He provides for our needs, even when others say that our simple faith is ridiculous. Trust Him to provide for what He's calling you to do.

Ministry in Northern Canada

II

WHEN WE ARRIVED, PEOPLE FROM THE CHURCH HAD BAGS AND BAGS OF groceries waiting for us at our house. Thank You, Jesus! I feel so spoiled!

The journey across Canada in summer was beautiful but often very hot. I confess that I was a little resentful at times. I was driving the car— which didn't have air conditioning—and I had to keep all the windows down for most of the trip because I was boiling. The dry prairie heat makes curly hair look awful. It's a good thing the only ones looking at me were the cat and her kittens. When we stopped for lunch and a break, Bill and the kids looked cool as cucumbers in the air-conditioned rental truck! Eventually Bill had to take the cat and the kittens, because even they were too hot! Anyway, we made it, and I'm thankful.

I really like this house we bought. It has a very smart layout. The kitchen is a good size. I even have a couch in the kitchen. It's that big! We have a few days to settle in before our first Sunday. We'd better make them count.

It was a great service today. This new church has a large sanctuary with three sections. Unfortunately we didn't get the full tour of the building before the service began. We had explained to our two-year-old and four-year-old why we needed them to sit nicely in church. I'm not sure they heard us.

When we were singing "How Great Thou Art," looking like a model family, I thought, I noticed that people around me were not singing but laughing. I thought to myself, *How ungodly!* Then I looked at our daughter. She was standing at the end of pew with her dress hiked up to her armpits, pulling her panties up and down in time to the music. I was beyond mortified. As if on cue, Martin knew it would be his turn next.

After dealing with that little untimely exhibition, it was time for the weekly announcements. What could possibly go wrong? Well, Martin began to talk very loudly. I honestly don't even know what he was saying. After being asked by his father to please be quiet, he loudly refused. Then Bill picked him up and began to carry him out of the service. I think all eyes were glued to the Bill and Donna Dyck Show.

Not far from where we were sitting was a door at the front of the sanctuary. In the midst of this crisis, Bill assumed that a closer exit would be better. Bad decision! As it turned out, the door at the front was only to a storage room. There was no staircase to the basement, as Bill had imagined. Out came Bill from the door at the front of the sanctuary, still carrying our boy. Martin was yelling as loud as he could, "Don't spank me!" I think even the hard of hearing took notice.

We were thoroughly humbled. I know kids are supposed to be a blessing. I really do think this is true—especially when they're sleeping. As for today, we lost count of how many people said, "It's good to know that you are just people like us." So, here we are, not feeling particularly exemplary. I wonder what the elders are thinking?

Tonight Bill and I talked for a while about our first experience at the new church. We know God called us here. We will need to trust Him to equip us—we will make mistakes, and so will our children.

When I look at Jesus' disciples, they seem to have been pretty rough around the edges. Yet Jesus still did great things through them. I'm praying that Jesus will do the same with us. He will lead and guide us. I know there are a few minefields ahead, and I know He'll help us navigate all of them.

There are days when I feel like a single mom. Bill is being encouraged to follow the senior pastor's pattern. He's paid for forty hours a week and donates another forty to the church. Eighty hours every week sounds insane to me.

I hope this eventually changes. I feel like we're living church. Our entire weekend is spent with the youth or college and career groups. They're all great people, but it would be nice to have a life with Bill that was beyond the church. I think this schedule is over the top, to be honest. Are all churches like this?

I'm thinking of starting a women's mid-week Bible study. I've asked the ladies, and they're very interested. So I think I'll try it. Childcare will be made available. That way I can bring my two kids.

There's a team of women willing to work alongside me in this new ministry. We'll think and pray about it more. We need to know what God wants us to do. Our plans might sound spiritual, but that doesn't make them right. We need to do what God is asking of us.

We had a great drive last night. I never thought I would see four moose all in one spot! We were told they go there every evening as the sun sets. We just sat there on the side of the road in the car and watched them. It was amazing!

People here eat moose meat. I've never heard of that before. A few very nice people gave us a lot of moose and elk meat. I'll have to learn how to cook it.

I'm thankful that God led us to this small city. I know there's a lot for me to learn. I need to come to terms with some things. I can't believe how much groceries cost. Once we pay the mortgage and the regular bills, we have just enough for groceries. The moose and elk meat will help. At least I don't have to buy meat! We're always trusting God to take care of us. So far, He always has.

Coming to grips with expectations is important because unmet expectations bring frustration later on. We who are in church ministry should not expect a lot of leisure time or riches. Contentment is critical—learning to be content in every situation, whether we have much or little. The key is that we can do all things through Christ who gives us strength.

—Philippians 4:11–13

Time goes quickly in ministry. It's crazy busy. I'm learning how to cook and clean quickly. I prefer meals and desserts that make people think I spent hours in preparation when in reality they come together quickly and easily.

Bill is enjoying being a pastor. He is, however, facing some challenges. When he leads the worship music from the piano, people complain and say that he needs to play louder. Others complain and tell him to play softer. Then there are those who want more hymns. Others speak up and tell Bill to cut back on the hymns. In light of all the requests, you would think that Bill is performing for these people rather than leading them in worshiping God. Honestly, I doubt much prayer preceded their comments. I'm worried that some things will never change, despite Bill's best efforts.

When Bill came home from work the other day, he was very quiet. I didn't know what was bothering him. Bill is careful about what kind of news he tells me because he knows that some things will make me really mad. I understand his silence. After a little while, I managed to get him to tell me that someone—the person's name was left out—said some really unkind and discouraging things to him. Now I have to figure out how to go to church and not wonder who it was. I know I would love to give him or her a piece of my mind! More and more, I'm beginning to understand why forgiveness is such a big deal in ministry. A person wouldn't have to be in ministry long before getting bitter if he or she didn't forgive.

Our women's Bible study is going really well. The participation has been amazing!

The people here are wonderful. On occasion, some folks from the church invite us to sit with them at their campfires in the evening. They laugh and bring out their guitars and sing while they drink coffee or tea. The kids run around and play. It's a lot of fun for all of us.

I just found out that I'm pregnant with our third child. I wondered why I've been feeling so tired. The kids are very excited. Martin has asked me if it's a boy, and if it is, could we please name him "Moses." Martin has been learning about Moses in Sunday school. I need to figure out how to tell Martin that Moses is not one of the names on my list.

Finances and ministry are tricky things—at least for us. For the most part, it doesn't bug me that we have so little money, but it would be nice to be able to fly home, back to Ontario, for Christmas. But because of our financial situation, it isn't even a consideration. There are no direct flights to Toronto, so we would each need two plane tickets each way. That would be four tickets round trip for each of us. It's out of the question. My mom said, though, that she wants to come here for a month. That would be really nice. We would have lots of fun, and she would love the people here. Bill always likes it when my mom visits. The food improves.

I met a very nice woman named Lucy, a mother of four. I can't imagine life with four children. It seems like an awful lot of work. She came for tea today. She told me about her husband, who has struggled with alcoholism for many years and is seldom home.

Her attitude was not one of complaining, but rather she just said it as it is—a challenge she faces. There was no bitterness in her. She relies on Christ in everything. I was very impressed by her. She reminded me not to be a complainer.

It's so easy to be a complainer. I knew that I couldn't complain to this woman about the frustrations I'm facing. Lucy is an overcomer. Through her story and her outlook on life, she challenged me to be an overcomer too.

A pastor's wife who whines must look and sound pretty bad to someone on the outside looking in. This is especially true considering that the Bible tells us to be content in every situation. I'm very good at complaining. I'm going to have to do some serious praying about this. Complaining pastors' wives are bad news! Furthermore, I don't want my kids to grow up to be complainers. I know they always listen to and watch me.

Complaining is a joy stealer for everyone—not just for the one doing the complaining but also for the one who has to listen. Paul, even while in prison, said to always be thankful. Never in Scripture are we given permission to complain. That's curious, because we're often very practiced in it.

This is our first Christmas here. It sure is busy! Mom is here and is having a great time. She loves it. She's really enjoying the kids. They're always very entertaining. She's been cooking up a storm. She even made Christmas cake, which Bill loves!

I'm excited about the new year. In June we will have a new baby, which is also pretty exciting. We look forward to meeting him or her; we still don't know if it will be a boy or girl.

I find it hard to know where to spend my time. There are so many women I can be friends with, listen and laugh with and care for. Yet I'm only one girl. Also, they're all Christians. I love the lost too! How should I be spending my time in the new year? Who should I be giving myself to?

I heard about a really cool ministry for adult children of alcoholics that I would love to be involved with. I would get to know some women who don't know Jesus and share how He's the healer of the broken-hearted. It's the next thing on my prayer list that I need God's direction on. I'll talk it over with Bill and see how he feels about it.

It's hard to believe that in a few months we will have been here for a whole year. It feels like only a few weeks have passed. The kids love it here. The backyard is huge, and they're always dreaming up some new adventure. A little while ago, Bill made a snow mountain with a great toboggan run that twists and turns. They spent hours on that thing. Their sleds go really fast and can even be steered, which is always handy!

One girl in the church told me a story about her three-year-old son. She had just put him in the yard to play. Their house is right in the centre of town, where it's quite busy. The fence surrounding the house is only about four feet high. She went inside, only for a moment, to make a cup of tea. She had barely got the water into the kettle when the Lord said very clearly to her, "Go and get your son!" She ran outside and was just in time to see a man grab her little boy. She pulled her boy out of his hands. Good thing she knows the Shepherd's voice and obeys it!

Another pastor's wife in town has become a very good friend. The only thing that bothers me is the crush she has on a fellow in her church. He's married, like she is. It just seems weird to me. I'm not sure what to say to her. In my years at Bible college and in all the reading I've done, I've never received any advice on this kind of matter. I'm going to talk to God about it. Honestly, I feel like I must not be hearing her correctly! The whole thing is just weird.

I feel rattled inside because of a woman who phoned me today in tears. She has five children, all in their twenties. It's a beautiful family. They've spent their entire lives as missionaries to First Nations people.

Today she told me that her daughter was killed by a drunk driver last year. The whole story was heartbreaking. She found out last week that the fellow who killed her daughter is getting out of prison today. She and her husband have not even gathered enough money for a headstone for their daughter's grave. The situation sounds extremely unfair. I didn't know what to say to her. I'm young and have never walked a path like that. I can't imagine losing a child, let alone losing one to a drunk driver.

She asked me, "Where is God in all this?" I wish I had a brilliant answer for her. Unfortunately, I don't! I know that some questions won't be answered until we get to heaven. Perhaps her question will be one of them. James says, "If any of you lacks wisdom, let him ask God" (James 1:5). That's exactly what I'm going to do.

The only One who can comfort this dear woman is God. That's what I'll pray, that God will comfort her. It's days like this when I feel inadequate for the position of pastor's wife. If pastors' wives are supposed to have all the answers, I'm clearly not doing well.

I've been thinking about our call to ministry. I know that Jesus called Bill and me to this ministry. I know from the many pastors' wives I've met over the years that some think only their husbands are called. They're not involved in the ministry at all. I'm not like that; I love ministry. If I had not married a pastor, I would be doing ministry anyway. I know that not every pastor's wife is the same. However, I continue to believe that God calls both partners into ministry. While the method and time required may differ between couples, the call that's placed on both remains.

I met one pastor's wife a while ago who left me with a few questions. She said she loves the church they're called to but hates the city where the church is located. That makes no sense to me. How effective can her ministry be if she hates the place she lives in? She says she loves the people in the church, but doesn't Jesus love the people in the mall and doctor's office also? Shouldn't we care for the people beyond the walls of our church? It's too bad I didn't have the courage to say what I thought to be true. Maybe no one else has ever challenged her thinking.

I met another pastor's wife last year who was very lonely. She didn't live near me, or I would have really been a friend to her. I asked her why she wasn't friends with the women in her congregation. She saw herself as set apart or different from the women in her church. She believed that they only wanted to be her friend because her husband was the pastor, not because of her own qualities. I wish I had a good comeback for her too, but I didn't. It has never occurred to me that anyone would befriend me simply because of my husband's position. I may be married to the pastor, but that doesn't mean that when people see me they think "Here's the pastor's wife!" Rather, I think they see me. The thoughts she struggles with have never crossed my mind.

The only time I'm bothered is when a woman from the church or community has an infatuation with my husband. Just because someone is a pastor doesn't mean he'll catch on right away. There have been times when I've had to help Bill see that a woman is paying a bit too much attention to him. He's not very aware of these matters. He wasn't even before we were married, though he did catch on when we met!

Once a woman was convinced that I had a mad crush on her husband. She was ready to leave him so he and I could start our new life together! What?

No thank you! I told her, "I have a husband whom I love, and you can have yours." I was in shock. It's made me very careful around married men. To be honest, I'm a little paranoid at times in this regard. I never did anything except talk to that guy! Anyway, I'm glad it's in the past. I'll let it stay there.

When one spouse is called, so is the other. How could it be otherwise? In marriage, God takes two people and makes them one. This doesn't mean they're both up front in leadership or that one isn't working in another job outside the church. Rather, the burden of the work that God has called them to falls upon both shoulders. Both feel it. Both embrace it. Both bring their respective gifts to the work and are intent on one goal. Neither runs from it. How it's lived out is usually quite different for each of them, but God's enabling for the call is also made available to both. It's like a sweater made for two. They will need that call when the ministry is difficult and they're deeply discouraged.

Our third child came in the middle of the night. It was bad timing, really. He was in such a big rush that the doctor didn't make it to the hospital on time. Thankfully, we did. There was a midwife on duty who delivered this beautiful baby boy. Unfortunately they couldn't find the laughing gas in time for the delivery, so I had the baby with no drugs or anything! I really like the gas, though, and I was mad they couldn't find it. Who loses something like that? My husband reminded me, now I could be a like pioneer mothers, who always gave birth without drugs. But I'm not a pioneer or a hero in any respect. I hear women talk about how they would never take drugs when delivering a baby. Well, that's wonderful. I prefer to not have pain in childbirth. Eve may have messed it up for me many centuries ago, but why suffer when I don't have to? Enough, I know. I'm done now.

The Sunday morning challenge—getting two young children and one baby out the door and to church on time by myself—is no small feat. Most weeks, I do somehow manage.

I love having company for lunch after church. Sunday company means, though, that on Saturday I have to clean and cook ahead. On Sunday the drill begins: dress everyone, try to look reasonable myself—you'd be amazed at just how fast a mother of young children can get her makeup on—throw a roast in the oven, and then remember to turn the oven on. Some people think that a roast is a lot of work. When I do it, I divide the labour. I get Bill to peel the potatoes and carrots. That's half the battle right there. Then I prepare what's left. It took me a while to master the whole operation, but we're pretty good now. I think it means a lot to be invited into someone's home for a meal. The kids love it and think there's something wrong when a Sunday goes by and we have no one coming over or we're not going somewhere.

> *Hospitality isn't the "job" of the pastor alone. Scripture says that everyone should seek to be hospitable (Romans 12:13). Perhaps that frightens you—please don't let it. People come to see you, not a perfect house or a perfect meal. I've served soup, hotdogs—people don't care. They just love being in your home, even for a bowl of ice cream. Keep it simple. Share what you have. We've enjoyed many years of visiting, in our own home, the people God has called us to minister to.*

Now that the kids are in bed and we've made it through the day, I need to get something straightened out. I was pretty upset after I got the three kids' winter stuff on and then got them out to the van, only to discover that it wouldn't and couldn't start. After I unloaded all the kids, I slammed the back door of the house so hard that a plaque fell off the wall. Ironically, it listed all the fruit of the Spirit—and I was clearly lacking in every department. I'm sure most pastors' wives would have gently shut the door and offered to teach the kids the Sunday school lesson at home, but the thought never crossed my mind.

I've been struggling to come to terms with the way Bill glows some days after church. I spend a lot of time in the nursery. During the week, I hang out with toddlers. In the mornings I get my toddlers dressed. Then in the evenings I get them to bed. My life is spent with toddlers. There's very little glowing in my life at the moment. In comparison, when Bill gets home from church or a prayer meeting, he looks a bit like he just walked down Mount Sinai after being with God. I'm trying to work on simply being happy for Bill. An attitude of gratitude would fit well into my life at the moment. I just needed to air my feelings for a minute. I *am* thankful for a beautiful husband and great children. It's not easy to find time to be quiet with Jesus these days. I need to work harder at it. Even a few minutes would help.

We live quite a distance from any store. The elders were coming over a few nights ago, and Bill asked me to make a special cake. I didn't run into any problems—until it came time to make the icing. Earlier that day, I had asked Bill to bring home some milk. He said he would, but his intended time of delivery was a long way away from when I needed it.

It was time to get creative. I looked through my fridge. Thankfully the cake recipe itself didn't call for milk, just the icing. I only needed half a cup. What to do?

Then it hit me: *I have milk. I'm breastfeeding! They'll never know.* I'm a pro now at expressing milk, so I got my measuring cup and had half a cup in no time. It couldn't have been more organic. I finished the cake and baked on the icing.

Later the elders started to arrive with their wives. Coffee and tea were waiting, along with my special cake. It was seriously impressive.

Everyone was gobbling it down when one of them asked for seconds. They commented on how delicious it was. "It has my own special touch," I said.

A look of quiet horror came over Bill's face. He remembered that I had asked him to buy milk, but the cake was finished when he got home with it. He almost spit the cake out of his mouth.

Not deterred, I got up and served them all a second piece. Bill, however, politely declined.

No one can say I'm not resourceful.

Today Bill came home troubled. Earlier in the day, when he got to work, he found a large unsigned message on the blackboard in his office. It said, "Does everything really happen because of prayer?" No name.

The note flowed out of a message Bill had preached recently, as well as the way he leads his ministry. I told him that there were worse notes he could find on his blackboard. In my heart, though, I wanted to examine the handwriting of everyone in the church, find out who did this, and ask why he or she didn't sign it.

Our senior pastor said he's received several unsigned and unkind letters over the years. So if there's no signature, he doesn't read the letter. I guess that's one way of dealing with it.

On the good-news front, Martin made a card for Bill. He told me exactly what to write, and then he drew a picture. He also signed it in his own way. The card listed many of Bill's qualities, including "He's waterproof." The things a three-year-old can think up! That made Bill smile.

We've had a lot of fun with baby Andrew. He's almost fourteen months old now. He's very cute, with his curly blond hair and big blue eyes. He's full of adventure.

I've felt off for weeks now. I thought I'd come down with some kind of lingering illness. I finally went to the drugstore and got a pregnancy kit. I did the test twice. I couldn't believe my eyes!

I can tell you this: never in a million years did I imagine I would be the mother of four children. I'm in shock! I find myself looking at other mothers of four to see how worn-out they look. Some look worse for wear than others. It's going to be difficult to maintain my present level of involvement in ministry once the new baby arrives.

That pastor's wife from the other church is continuing to get herself in pretty deep with another man. I don't know what to do. She doesn't seem to see this as a problem! It's making it very difficult for me to be with her. She said that she confessed her sin to me, and that's good enough. But the sin isn't against me—it's against her husband. This is very stressful! I need to take some time to ask God for wisdom. What am I supposed to do? I feel like I'll wreck their ministry if I say anything. I can't ask anyone around here for advice. I wish there was a book about what to do when a pastor or his wife is found cheating. I would read it.

After a lot of thinking and praying I decided on a course of action regarding this other pastor's wife. I told her again that she needed to tell her husband. But once more she refused. She said she would go to her grave with this secret. That was not the response I was looking for.

So, I moved to step two. This involved my calling their superiors in her denomination. I felt like I was destroying their ministry. Yet I couldn't stand seeing her messing around behind her husband's back. I was in tears talking to the man who was on the other end of the line. Honestly, I was so torn. The leader said to tell her that if she didn't confess fully to her husband by six this evening, then he'll tell him. I was even more terrified telling this woman what will happen if she doesn't come clean with her husband. I don't think there has been a conversation in my lifetime that I've dreaded more than this one.

When I saw her later this afternoon, I had to explain my conversation with her husband's superior, and she was furious with me, as I knew she would be. She called me many nasty names. What a day! I never want to live through this again!

She ended up telling her husband by the appointed hour. Now the situation will be handled properly.

As much as I didn't want to speak up, I knew I had to. It wasn't right to remain silent in this situation, though it would have been a more comfortable course of action. I'm praying that Jesus will bring healing to that marriage.

This fourth baby came in a hurry. The good thing about giving birth to a fourth baby is that labour goes quickly. He was born one hour after the first contraction. I'm happy to report that they found the laughing gas. I made sure of it.

I was hoping he would be a she, as we already have two boys. I thought that another girl would bring a good balance to the family. And I'm out of boy names. As a result, Bill began to pray about a name. I know that I should be more involved in the process, but frankly, I'm just happy to be resting once more.

Bill chose the name "Michael," and we're all thankful for him. Now I need to figure out life as a mother of four. I've heard that the only difference between having three children and four is that with three you almost catch up and with four you never do. I don't know how Bill's mom did it with seven.

I'm very tired. It's so nice to have Bill's parents here. Dad is building a tree-house for Martin and a playhouse for Lisa. He likes to have a project when he comes. Last time it was a picnic table. The kids will love it. Bill is being ordained while his parents are here. It's exciting. We'll have a big celebration when he passes.

I'm grateful for the friendships I have here. There are many great people in this northern town, but I don't have any spare time when I can get to know more of them. This causes me to feel guilty at times. I want to help everyone, but I know I can't.

I've come to the realization that I can't rescue people or fix them. That's Jesus' work, not mine. Clearly, we must be faithful to what God calls us to do and helpful among the people we're called to serve. We need to be wise and discerning in this matter.

After answering the phone, I wished I hadn't picked it up. That pastor's wife who was cheating on her husband hates me now. She said some pretty horrible things to me on the phone. She was accusing me of judging her again. She told me I'm emotionally unwell and very selfish. I can't remember what else.

The tears on my face may have dried, but the words spoken feel like steak knives cutting into my heart.

I know I need to forgive her. I'm not quite ready to do that yet. I'm hurting on the inside still. I'll forgive, however. Becoming bitter isn't an option. It would disqualify me from ministry. Also. Jesus doesn't give me the option of not forgiving.

I need the Lord to show me if there's something I need to apologize for. I'm very quick to feel guilty, whether or not I'm actually in the wrong. I need Jesus to soothe my aching soul.

I've learned that sometimes people in ministry can behave badly. That's an unexpected lesson for me.

It's very important to guard your heart against bitterness. It sneaks its way into your soul like a rotten cold. It poisons your perspective, and its bite is felt in the way you speak. Eventually it disqualifies an individual from ministry, until he or she forgives. A hard but important lesson.

I've been thinking about Ontario a lot. I miss being near family, especially *my* family. Mom has been really sick. This Christmas we're flying home, thanks to an unexpected financial gift. We haven't been home for two years, and that feels like a long time. I can't wait to see everyone, and

I would love to move back. Bill said he isn't even remotely interested in doing ministry in Ontario. He said God will have to make it painfully obvious to him if that's His will.

Well, we'll see. I'm praying for the painfully obvious, if that's what it takes.

We've had a wonderful time with family and friends over Christmas. It was hard to see my mother so sick. You wouldn't believe what happened!

The children and I stayed for an extra week so I could have a little more time with my mom. I tried one last time to convince Bill to put his resumé in with the Ontario district. But he gave me the same response— no. Then came the plane ride back to northern Canada.

When Bill boarded the plane, he sat down beside a Christian minister in Toronto. In fact, he was a member of the same denomination as us. He and Bill chatted all the way. And before he got off the plane, he offered Bill a position at his church!

After three days of fasting and praying, Bill knew what God wants us to do. It's time to go back to Ontario! I get excited when I think about it. Bill said we'll likely move this coming summer. We'll finish the ministry year here and then head back to Ontario and find out what God has for us.

I still think it's funny that Bill met that pastor. It's unusual to sit beside a Christian on a plane, let alone a pastor in your denomination in the city your wife just asked you about. It's also strange that Bill was offered a job in that exact city. That's something only God could line up. These events have His fingerprints all over them.

Bill submitted his letter of resignation. We'll be leaving in a few months. My only regret will be to leave all the really great friends I've made up here. There are some amazing people in this town. I'm sad to be saying goodbye to them soon.

Our house is listed for sale. Once again, we need a miracle. Good thing the God we serve is also the God of miracles. This town is based on a boom-and-bust market, following the trends of the oil industry. At times there can be a ton of houses for sale. We have a real estate agent, but Bill and I know that selling houses, at least for us, is God's business.

As it turns out, we won't be taking a new pastoral position right away. Bill will take the next two years to go to seminary. We now have nine years in ministry altogether. We believe we need to take this opportunity to learn, and perhaps rest. So the money from the house is all we'll have to live on. We will need the equity to support us as Bill returns to school.

A woman from our church asked me, "What makes you so sure God will sell your house?" She said many people have been waiting a long time for their houses to sell. I told her, "We don't have a long time. We have four weeks. That's it. The money in that house is all the money our family has to live on. The house *has* to sell."

So we will move with our four small kids, one cat, and the dog, Moses. A little yellow house with a crabapple tree in the backyard will be our next home. Small houses have the potential to make you crazy—or more organized. I'm hoping that I'll become more organized. I'm already a bit crazy!

I find it humorous how God seems to wait until the last minute to answer the prayers of His people.

Today is the last day for the sale of the house. All the paperwork has to be submitted. Only a few people have come to see our house. We replaced all the cupboard knobs in the kitchen, which sounds insignificant. It was expensive! I couldn't believe how much it cost. Why I thought new knobs would help sell the house is a mystery to me, but, I must confess, it was my idea.

The doorbell rang around four this afternoon. When I opened the door, there stood a woman from our church. She said, "God told me I'm supposed to buy your house. How much are you asking?" I was astounded, to say the least. I told her, and she asked if she could take a look around and see what she was buying. She didn't like my decorating or even the new knobs I had put on the cupboard doors as I was trying to help Jesus. He clearly didn't need the knobs replaced in order to sell the house.

She went straight down to the realtor's office and wrote a cheque in the amount of our asking price. Not a penny more or less. The realtor said in twenty-five years that has never happened to her.

Bill got a little bit upset with me during our trip. We have a huge van. You can see us coming for quite a distance.

We were travelling across the prairies with the windows open. Getting four kids to sleep in a van on a long journey is difficult, but the kids were all snoring. A huge green bug flew in the window and landed right on my arm. I screamed and jumped out of my seat, right on top of two sleeping children. That quickly ended the sleeping, but it started the crying. Bill was not happy with me. "It's just a bug!" he said. I don't like bugs. Especially big green ones on my arm!

Two Years of Seminary

III

I'm so relieved to have the opportunity here at seminary to just *be* for the first time in our married lives. We will sit on the receiving end and enjoy being taught.

I love our little yellow house. It's going to be just fine. Our kids are excited. There are a lot of pools in this city, which is good, because Lisa and Martin love swimming. We'll see how Andrew feels about it. Michael's a little too young to care.

I was thinking how difficult it is to see clearly at times in ministry. In our last ministry position, I honestly didn't know how to deal with some of the troubles we encountered. Being the worship music leader, Bill lost much of his joy in leading people in worship because of criticism.

People forget that they come to church to worship God, not comment and complain about their preferences. I give these people over to God. I pray He'll bring the joy of worship back to Bill and help us both forgive, from the heart, the many people who complain with such freedom.

I'm thankful for new days. Thank You, God, for these two years of reprieve we have before we head back into ministry.

I'm thankful for this new adventure. I love meeting all the people here. There are some amazing servants in God's Kingdom. What a privilege we have to meet them!

I'm going to see a counsellor here at seminary. She and her husband have been in ministry for a long time. I need to unpack the years we spent up north. Maybe growing up in my family has left me mixed up and blind to some of the issues I faced. I always felt like God and I had done a lot of work in this department over the years. Perhaps there's still a bit more work to be done.

It will be good to sit with this woman and have the opportunity to tell someone my story of growing up in an alcoholic home. Yet, much more than that, I want to find out if I'm as self-centred and emotionally unwell as that other pastor's wife said I am. I don't want to be like that. I'm asking Jesus to help me see the truth. I can't fix or work on something I don't admit is a problem.

Then I want to talk to the counsellor about what happened with that pastor's wife.

We all need to sit before the King and ask Him to heal the broken and bruised parts of our hearts. We're all works in progress. God does not look for perfect people, just people who are willing to be honest and open with Him. When we look at the motley crew who were Jesus' disciples and what He did through them, we should all be encouraged!

I really like my seminary class in pastoral methods. The whole class is men, except for me. Bill seems to be enjoying all of his classes. I bring candies to mine. My friend keeps falling asleep, so I throw candies at him when the professor isn't looking. I see it as a ministry to the poor guy. It helps keep him awake.

Today's discussion was interesting. The other students talked about how they tell their wives everything that happens with people in their ministries. They said their wives are their number-one confidantes.

It sounds good in practice, but in real life, I told them, it's not neces-sarily the wisest decision. I shared with them a personal experience from when Bill and I were first married. Bill was working for Youth Unlimited and was also the bookkeeper for the church we attended. He didn't tell me much about the bookkeeping. I didn't care about the numbers, because they mean very little to me. Well, this church had a big problem, and Bill pointed it out to them. Every organization that receives donations must have a charitable number so they can issue tax receipts. Apparently, their charitable number was not current and had not been for a few years, which is a serious oversight. I had no idea. I honestly didn't even know then exactly what a charitable number is.

A knock came to our door, and when I opened it, there was an elder from the church, accusing me of gossiping about this problem with the charitable number. I had no idea what he was talking about. Bill confirmed it when he told the man that he had told me nothing.

I've never been so thankful for my husband's tight-lipped approach. I didn't need to know. He protected me.

As I look back over our last ministry position, I appreciate that Bill only told me what I needed to know. It can be hard to worship standing beside people who you know are big critics of your husband's ministry. I didn't need to know, and I didn't want to know. It's not that Bill told me nothing. He only told me the bottom line, and that was enough for me. I think that wives who are told everything are given a great weight to bear, which can, at times, become unprofitable.

I've never met so many pastors' wives in my life. The student wives fellowship is a lot of fun. They know how to laugh. I see how very different we all are. Some are outgoing. Some are very fashionable. Others are very good at saving money. Some are funny, and others are very serious. Yet God called them all into ministry. He'll use all of the many gifts He's given to these women.

I'm amazed by the variety. Some leave me a bit mystified though. They put us in small groups of three. I went to my first one, and honestly, I'm not sure I'll go back.

These women have kids older than mine, but that's not the issue. The problem is that they struggle with depression and spent most of the time sharing their complaints about pretty much everything. I didn't know how to contribute. I'm as good at complaining as anyone, but I've worked hard to not be a complainer—especially with women I just met ten minutes before.

Complaining comes pretty easily really, but it's far from life-giving. I was almost silent. I'm thankful they have each other to talk to. I'm a few years younger than both of them. I could challenge them to see things differently, but I don't feel it would be well received. I've never struggled with depression, so what can I say? I don't know for sure that depression is even the primary issue. I was, however, feeling depressed when I drove home—that much I do know.

I was thinking today that, as much as there are different pastors' wives, there are different pastors. Some are super outgoing, and others are quiet, like Bill. Yet God works through them all.

The other day, Bill and I were at a young married couples' event. We were doing an activity where every couple defined their relationship. Bill felt like he had an epiphany. He told everyone, "Donna makes people like us, and I make people believe us." He thought that was brilliant. Maybe it was a bit true, I have to admit!

Bill and another pastor are working in the church nursery with the two- to three-year-olds. Bill loves it, and our Andrew is in his class. I never knew that working with toddlers could bring so much refreshing to someone!

The kids are having a great time here. Winter is *freezing*! Other than that, we're good. Bill is struggling with Greek. He's been failing the class. He told me one morning that while he was up early, as is his custom, and praying for missionaries, right in the middle of his prayer God showed him a page of Greek in a vision. Then God showed Bill the pattern in the Greek language. Bill said it has helped so much! Now he's doing really well in Greek. He should be—I've never heard of God tutoring students in Greek before.

We packed up the van and our four young children and began the drive across Canada, heading to Ontario for Christmas. The weather was bitterly cold and snowy.

After we had been driving for many hours, we needed gas and a break for supper. The towns were few and very far between. It was late and the weather was awful when we entered one town. Suddenly the van stalled— right in front of a gas station and a motel. We thought, "Wow, God is good! We ran out of gas right in front of a gas station!" But it was worse than that. The van would not start even after we got gas.

The gas attendent called the local mechanic, who had left for the day. He came to look at our van and discovered that the fuel pump was shot. He didn't have one in stock and would have to order it. It would take several days to arrive. That was a big problem, as it was a Friday, and we wouldn't be able to continue our journey until the following week! Not to mention, we couldn't afford this new problem!

The mechanic thought about it and then said, "I have a race car at home, and it uses the same size fuel pump. I'll go home and take it off. I can install it tomorrow for you, and you can be on your way." We were so thankful.

We stayed at the nearby motel and were on the road the next day by one p.m. We talked about all the ways God met us on this trip. The van could have stalled anywhere, but God knew and was watching over us. When we left that town, we found that the next town was hours away. We felt very cared for by our Heavenly Father.

Today I had my last session with the counsellor. In one of our previous sessions, she had me do some tests. Today I received the results. I'm not quite as pathetic as my friend from the north country said I am. That's good news. The counsellor interpreted the results and said that I see myself honestly. Overall, I'm deeply encouraged by all she had to say. I know what I need to do next.

Classes are drawing to a close soon. Now we need to find a ministry position.

It's interesting to hear the different ways people feel God is leading them. Some feel led to a particular part of the country. Others feel a calling to go overseas. A few decided to do what seems most logical. God leads them all. There's no set formula God uses to lead His people. Every story is unique. The way God burdens people's hearts for a ministry or place is incredible.

Bill and I know God wants us in Ontario. We both believe, more specifically, that this is to be in Toronto. God is in control. He will lead us. He will open and close doors according to His plan.

In the meantime, God will provide for us. He has to, or we'll be in big trouble!

Bill got a call from a church up in Thunder Bay. It's in northern Ontario and not what we had in mind. Furthermore, the position isn't what we were hoping for. Bill said the senior pastor is wonderful. Even still, neither of us believe this is the position God has for us. This waiting part of life isn't always easy, and I'm not known for my patience. I know that I need to trust God with all of our needs.

The kids know we're moving. It's hard to prepare them, because we don't know exactly where we're going. I often feel as if I'm standing in the middle of a forest, waiting for a pathway that leads me from here to there—the place I'm supposed to be. This path in the middle of a forest is how I see life. I can, however, take comfort in the knowledge that God is leading me down the right path. This is what "walking by faith and not by sight" looks like. Right now, we're walking entirely by faith, and so are many of our colleagues from seminary.

A few weeks ago, our son Martin heard Bill and me describing his class. The entire class, except for Martin, is made up of First Nations children. Well, Martin went back to school the next day and checked. When he got home, he informed us that he's exactly like all the kids in his class. We didn't argue with him. He also insisted that his teacher's name is Miss Vain. I told him he was wrong; her name is actually Miss Bane. He, however, continued to call her Miss Vain—until she finally corrected him. He humbly came home today and informed me that I was right. Always a joy to know you're right, even with a five-year-old.

I saw some of the resumés of other people who are applying for ministry positions. They look a lot cooler than Bill's. I told him that maybe he should make his resumé look a little more attractive. He refused. I guess whoever calls us will not be someone who's won over by an impressive-looking resumé.

We received a call from a small church in the heart of Toronto. The position is with a two-year-old church plant. Their congregation has a total of thirty people. One of Bill's friends told me the same church called him, but he turned down the opportunity. I asked him why. He said he didn't want to put his family through the difficulties and challenges of living in downtown Toronto. That made me worry. Are we nuts for considering this opportunity?

Bill told me the pay is pretty low, but we've already learned to live on very little. If God wants us there, I know He'll make a way. I can't say that raising my children in the heart of the city was ever a dream for me. This is yet another thing I must trust God in. God will have to step into the middle of all this. I don't even know how much it costs to live in downtown Toronto. We don't have much to put down on a mortgage anymore. We used most of our money to live on during the last two years!

This morning, I was reading my Bible and trying to listen to God. I felt like He asked me, "What will it take for you to feel safe raising your kids in downtown Toronto?"

I told Him, "Since You're asking, this is what I would need: I would like a house on a dead-end street. I need four bedrooms on one floor and two bathrooms, because there are six of us. I would love a fireplace, if You don't mind. We need a room for a church office, because they have no church building. I would like English-speaking neighbours. I don't mind if they speak other languages, but at least some English. Then, Jesus, I would really appreciate a park on our street for our children. Lastly, I would like to send our children to a Christian school."

The church in Toronto sounds very interested in us. We have had two phone interviews. They want us to fly down there in two weeks.

Bill and I are off to Toronto, where we will meet the people of this young church in the heart of the city. The current pastor and his wife will be leaving for the mission field. That's why the position became available. Apparently we're supposed to go look at houses while we're there. We're doing a lot of praying and trusting that God will show us what He wants.

Toronto is a big and busy city. It's much the way I remember from my childhood. I've never lived downtown. I always lived in Scarborough. Bill grew up near Niagara Falls. The city, especially the inner city, is foreign to him. We're excited though. It's a city deeply in need of the Lord Jesus.

When we were driving down Queen Street, something stood out to me. There's a bar not far from where the church meets. It's all black with an upside-down cross on the doorway. I don't think the people who go into that bar are there to worship God—that's for sure.

We feel a deep burden for this city. We know that the only way a church could thrive in the heart of this city is if God Himself did it. If we were to come here, God would be doing the work through us. Ministry in the urban core is far too difficult for anyone to do in his or her own strength.

An interesting collection of people attends this church. They're very nice, to be sure. We felt instantly at home with the congregation. They're a small group, and they're very warm to us.

The current pastor and his wife are really amazing. They will make incredible missionaries. They're people who believe, without question, that nothing is impossible with God.

We looked at houses. We're at the bottom of the market, for sure. The houses here are expensive, and we will need God's provision to buy one. Unfortunately, the salary is so low that we can't afford to rent a house. To make matters worse, we don't make enough to qualify for a mortgage. We will see what God does, as, humanly speaking, Bill and I know it's impossible.

We saw one house on a dead-end street. It has everything I asked for. God will have to keep it from selling until we know what we're going to do. I think houses sell quite fast in Toronto, especially downtown. I'm once again reminded that God is big enough to keep this one from selling. If we take this ministry position, we won't start for another two months.

We had a good flight back. We've prayed for days now about this little church and believe that Toronto is what God has in mind for us. It makes little sense, really. Financially, it will be very challenging, but I'm able to live pretty cheaply.

God has always been faithful. If He wants us in Toronto at this little church, He must create a way for us. So, we will see. We would start in July. Bill is calling them today. We'll have two months to get organized. We'll leave for Ontario when Lisa and Martin are finished school at the end of June.

They seemed excited that we decided to come. It will be wonderful to live near to our families once more—for the first time in seventeen years. The packing has begun. There's nothing like packing for a move to make you rethink what is worthy of keeping. Bill and I are deciding what furniture we can take with us. The houses in downtown Toronto, at least the ones we looked at, are not big.

> *All ministry, regardless of where God calls us, must be done in His strength and with the leading of His Spirit. It's easy to become dependent on our own strength, but we're taught in Scripture to simply rely on God. "If you abide in me, and my words abide in you, ask whatever you wish, and it will be done for you" (John 15:7). This is the key to fruitfulness—intimacy with Him and dependence upon Him.*

The packing is done, and the truck is coming. We're ready to go. I'm happy that the kids are excited for the long trip. They have their activity kits all ready to go. We have a two-day drive ahead of us.

The first thing we will do when we get to Toronto is put all our furniture and boxes in storage. We need to find a house. We'll find out if the house on the dead-end street is still on the market. I pray that it is.

Ministry in Downtown Toronto

IV

WHILE WE WERE UNLOADING OUR FURNITURE AT THE STORAGE PLACE, right off of Queen Street, we heard shouting and saw a young couple fighting. The man was pushing an empty stroller, while the woman was carrying a baby. The man took the stroller and was about to hit the woman with it! She started yelling, "Watch out for the baby!" Suddenly he stopped. We couldn't believe it. Lisa, only eight years old, said, "Mom, I'm glad God asked Dad to bring us to Toronto. These people need God."

We looked at so many houses today that I lost count. There's one that I remember—the house on the dead-end street is still on the market! It's the perfect house. It has everything I prayed for. We will put an offer in for this house later today. Bill is going to talk to someone about lending us some money so we can place a down payment. There's no other way. We're about $60,000 short of what we need. God will make a way. Once again, He has to.

We went and saw the only Christian school in downtown Toronto. The school looks amazing. The only problem is that the monthly tuition fee is more than Bill makes in a month. I'm going to have to tell the principal that we can't afford to send our kids there.

God made a way! Bill's parents gave us the $60,000 we needed for the house. Thank You, Jesus. The offer was accepted, and we move into our new home in four weeks. Thank You for Bill's very generous and kind parents.

While we were moving into our house, the phone rang. It was the principal of the Christian school. We had told her that we couldn't send our kids to her wonderful school, as it was financially impossible. She called to say she had spoken to her board and had received permission to invite our children to attend the school for free!

God has given us everything I asked for. He faithfulness shines through once more.

Bill's first full day of work at Toronto Alliance Church was certainly memorable. At some point in the day, a woman phoned him. She said she's a witch and needs deliverance from demons. She plans to be at church on Sunday.

The church meets in the basement of a school just off Queen Street West. At the moment, Bill is the worship team. He's also the preacher. It's like the Bill Dyck Show. There are very few children in the congregation. We'll need to figure something out for our kids. It seems, however, that the adults are their friends. Lisa and I are the coffee-and-tea department. We serve refreshments after every service. We all set up the chairs. Because of the refreshments service that we provide, Lisa and I don't have to put them away.

When we drove to church today, we found the reality of life in the downtown sadly unbelievable. Usually evil and depravity of human life are somewhat hidden. Today, however, it felt as though they were flaunting themselves before our eyes. The prostitutes were out early. They already appeared to be high and were looking for business. Homeless people begging for money seemed to be everywhere we looked. There was one fellow stripping on the sidewalk. After church, there was a fight outside a coffee shop. There was no shortage of yelling going on. We were reminded of the mission given to us by God.

At times, Bill and I have felt overwhelmed by the task at hand. The spiritual battles over recent months seem countless. Clearly, Toronto is a city the enemy is quite fond of. He'll not give it up without a fight.

I'm encouraged by 2 Corinthians 2:14, which reminds me, "Thanks be to God, who in Christ always leads us in triumphal procession."

Bill was leading worship music today and wasn't looking at the people at all. I couldn't figure out what his problem was. Later he told me a woman in the second row was breastfeeding her baby the whole time and didn't have anything covering herself. He said it was very difficult to know where to look. So he just looked at his keyboard.

I'm happy to report that we got a kitten. I've been cat-free for too many years. Bill gave in rather easily, but his lack of affection for cats hasn't changed. She's another calico kitten. Bill named her "Rahab." He feels it's an accurate name for a female cat. The rest of us call her "Speckles."

The witch lady—or so she claims—comes to every meeting. She's exhausting. The kids don't know what to think of her. They're not alone in this. It's times like these when the gift of discernment becomes a big deal. It's one thing to be kind and loving and another to be wise. Daily we pray and ask God for wisdom. We've never encountered anyone like her. Recently she became upset with Bill when he failed to respond to her exact requests. Two nights ago she called and asked him to go to her apartment and pray for her. I told him there was no way it would be wise for him to go alone. So he took along another fellow from the church. She was furious he didn't come alone. That confirmed in my mind that it's a good thing he *didn't* go alone! It's true that she's troubled by evil spirits. It's also true that she doesn't want Jesus. That's a problem, because He's the only one who can save her from evil spirits.

My neighbour keeps asking me to go with her to this moms' thing. She asks me every time I see her. I asked her for more details. She said it's at the Baptist church just down the street. So, I called the Baptist church and asked, "What is this MOPS thing all about?" The woman on the phone told me that it's a low-key evangelistic outreach for moms in the neighbourhood. It seems funny to me that my neighbour, who to the best of my knowledge isn't a believer, is inviting me, a pastor's wife, to a low-key evangelistic outreach program. She couldn't stop telling me about the many wonderful people who attend MOPS. I'm going to go with my friend next week. I'll take my boys along. They're always excited to meet more kids. I could certainly do with meeting a few more moms.

Old houses are not without their challenges. First, our cat had kittens, and second, Bill just destroyed a wasps' nest on the outside of our home. His accomplishment would sound impressive were it not for the fact that the wasps decided to come *into* our house, now that their outside home had been removed. There were hundreds of them. This morning I thought we had a demon loose in our living room, only to discover that a wasp had stung the orange kitten. This poor five-week-old kitten was howling as if under the influence of something evil. I found the lump on the poor kitten's head and, not far off, the dead wasp. Had it not happened at four in the morning, it wouldn't have been such a heart-stopping situation. A wasp stung me on the neck at six, in my own bed. I refuse to sleep in that room until this problem is truly solved.

We had the whole church over. You know your church is small when they all fit in your small house. We served tea and coffee, and a wasp fell into a woman's tea. She was very gracious about it. Soon after, Bill informed me that he was now officially at war with the unwelcomed wasps.

We were told that a new pastor will be joining us. He'll be Bill's assistant. He's a nice guy, but a bit on the wild side if you ask me. He and Bill couldn't be more opposite. His wife seems very nice and not as wild as her husband. They have two kids, which means our Sunday school program just increased 40 percent.

It frustrates me when we go to district events and visit with other pastoral couples from surrounding churches. They're great people for sure. They always ask us, "How big is your church?" I have a hard time telling them that we're up to forty-four people and have lost several along the way. It makes me feel like a failure, except I know in my head that the size of the church doesn't mean it's thriving. In response to my frustration and difficulty, Bill said that God asks us to be faithful to His calling. So I'll work on believing that.

We were visiting with a pastor and his family one Friday evening. That was a lot of fun. They're also church planters, from just outside of Toronto. They're finding things as tough as we are. They have four kids as well, and the kids had a great time together.

Bill was telling the pastor about this "witch" woman who has attended every church meeting for the last several months and how we're finding her exhausting. The shocker was this: they asked us her name, and they know her! They described her exactly and told us that they met her in Alberta. She had been to many of the churches there with the same story. She poses as a cripple and comes in a wheelchair. They told us she walks fine and that this is all an act. What? I knew things were not right with this woman. She's even used up all of Bill's patience, and that isn't easy to do. He's the most patient and kind person I've ever known. The pastor gave Bill excellent advice, and he'll act on it.

Last night we heard yelling on our street. The people down the road were all drunk. One of them was a mother with a very young baby in her arms as she and the father fought. Lisa even woke up when she heard the screaming. It was pouring rain outside, and there, in the middle of the downpour, were these people with their baby. The man was yelling and threatening to kill the woman.

I told Bill, "Jesus wouldn't stand by and watch from the window." Bill put on a pair of jeans and a T-shirt and then went outside into the rain. As soon as they saw him, they stopped. We had talked many times to these people, and they know Bill is a pastor. Anyway, within a few minutes the police came. Bill stood with the husband until he was taken away. It was a very sad night. Lisa and I sat down and prayed for these people while all of it was happening.

Some people may not want their kids to see things like this, but it's real life. It was an opportunity to go to the One who deeply cares for the brokenness around us. We know He's big enough. I want my kids' hearts to be broken over the sadness of people's lives and not repelled by it.

Bill and the older kids went out to feed the homeless tonight. Michael and I stayed home, as he's still too little. The kids really enjoyed it. Bill told me that one man refused to take a lunch from him. Four-year-old Andrew asked his dad to let him try. This man was sitting down, leaning against a building. Bill said the gentleman was very fearful. Andrew, with his curly blond hair and big blue eyes, crouched down to the man's eye level and said, "My daddy would never do anything to hurt you; take the lunch, sir. You must be hungry." The man took it. He said he had a bunch of friends in the alley, and he got them all. The kids and Bill gave out the last of the lunches and then returned home.

That story warmed my heart deeply. I know that Jesus cares very much for these people, regardless of why they're on the street. I'm glad the kids could go with their dad.

I had a dream last night about a woman. She was holding a three-headed snake. One of the snake heads lunged toward me and bit me. I trust that Jesus will give me wisdom to navigate whatever is before me.

God gives to His servants what is needed for His work. God gave Bill and me prophetic warnings throughout our ministry. They didn't strike fear in me as much as they provided me with a sense of caution and a call to prayer. God is faithful.

When I opened the mail today, there was a personal note from a woman in the church. I thought we were good friends. I enjoy her very much. She informed me that I'm "a real disappointment as a pastor's wife." She went on to explain that statement in some detail and mention a few other issues. I only read the letter once. I went to the Lord and talked about it with Him until my heart stopped pounding.

I called my sister-in-law—a beautiful Christian who loves me enough to be painfully honest. That was what I needed. After reading the letter to her, I asked if she felt there was truth to those words. Following a moment of silence, she said, "No, Donna. That's *not* true." Then I tore up the letter and threw it away. When the letter was destroyed, I could only remember the first thing the lady said, that I'm a disappointment. I would apologize to her if I could understand what God would have me say. At this point I'm just working on forgiving her. I since found out she and her husband have decided to leave the church, and two other women will join them. Evidently, they all feel the same.

I feel like I'm wrecking this ministry. I know I'm different than most pastors' wives. I often say what I think. Maybe I speak my mind too frequently. I need to learn to shut up sometimes and have better discernment. Something in me needs to change.

Bill came home today and told me about a letter the district superintendent received. It was written by the husband of the woman who sent me the letter. This letter to the superintendent described his deep concern over Bill's inability as a pastor and said that he was off theologically, among other things. Bill asked the superintendent what he was going to do about it. "Nothing, Bill; I threw it in the garbage. It's ridiculous." That was a relief.

I see again how very good you need to be at forgiving people if you want to stay in ministry. Fellow Christians can bring great hurt to us. I do know that it's *not* God leading these people. May Jesus heal our hearts and help us to keep our boots on.

It was a beautiful morning. We often sit on our front deck and have breakfast with our four kids. I love that. We had just said grace, as is our custom, when our neighbour poked his head around the corner of our deck. He said, "I just want you to know that we can tell you are Christians."

I replied, "Why, because you just heard us say grace?"

"No!" he said. "I've watched you live."

We were humbled, to say the least. We're also thankful, even though some of our Christian brothers and sisters may have disagreed with him. Our neighbour's words this morning were very healing for our discouraged hearts.

Church attendance was really low today. There were only twelve people, and six of the attendees were from our family. Most pastors would have quit by now. However, Bill is convinced that God has called us. We will be faithful to His calling.

To be honest, I feel like a failure. I've heard stories about other church planters. It sounded like their church plants grew in a matter of minutes. Another church plant that's going to open shortly out of one of the very large churches in our denomination is starting with 200 people! When Toronto Alliance Church was planted, it only started with a handful. Now, after just over two years, we're at twelve. That's not very good church growth.

This was our daughter Lisa's prayer last night: "Oh God, be with the homeless on the streets tonight. Help them not to freeze to death. And, oh God, help there not be any fires in Toronto this evening. I know there probably will be, but stay in charge, God. And God, help Mike Harris to not make so many cuts, especially with hospitals and the poor people."

On the funny side, though, our youngest son shaved off both eyebrows today. He looks hilarious. He'll certainly make his teachers smile tomorrow.

I've started a new ministry for addicts based on the twelve-step program from Alcoholics Anonymous. While I'm not and have never been an alcoholic or addict, I have dearly loved two alcoholics in my life: my father and my brother. Alcohol destroyed both their lives.

We had four men at our first meeting. One said to me, "You *must* have some kind of addiction." I told him honestly that it was not my journey—I just care deeply for them in theirs. If I have more than three chocolate chip cookies in a row I feel sick. That's as close as I come.

I love the honesty of these guys. It's beautiful. They don't need convincing that they need God to help them overcome their addictions.

Bill and I learned the hard way that compassion is a very poor leader.

One young man who attends the group struggles with alcohol and drugs. Bill and I invited him over for supper. We learned that he loves to play guitar. When he asked to borrow one of Bill's guitars, we foolishly lent it to him. We're too nice sometimes.

It was a valuable handmade guitar. It was too late when we realized that we will never see that guitar again, or him. That was the guitar Bill used every Sunday to lead the worship music.

Sam, one of the fellows in the addictions group, has been recovering from crack cocaine and alcohol. I introduced him to Bill, and they've become friends. Bill led him to faith in Jesus, and he has a beautiful faith. He phones Bill and leaves messages—many of them. Each time, Sam sings simple songs of thanksgiving he's made up for God. He's so thankful for the way that God is restoring his life.

Sam stopped by our house yesterday. I had made a pie for Bill. That in itself was unusual, as I don't like making pie. It turned out that I was feeling extraordinarily kind in the moment. In Sam's hand was a lemon meringue pie he had bought. He had eaten one piece and had enjoyed it so much that he wanted to share it with all of us. Gifts from people who have very little and yet are so generous humble me deeply.

Our youngest son, Michael, is in grade one now. He came home today and informed us that we needed to buy the cook at school a new gold watch, since hers was stolen. We asked him, "How would we afford a gold watch?"

Michael said, "Daddy, you always tell me we're filthy rich!" It's true that Bill often says this. Now he had some explaining to do. Bill told Michael what kind of riches he meant. He then contacted the cook at school and explained that we unfortunately can't buy the replacement gold watch. Poor Michael.

I've become deeply discouraged. Even as I'm praying for God to bless this ministry, the only churches that seem to be thriving are the big ones.

I was at a meeting with all the district churches. The district superintendent asked all these people who were seeing God do great things to share. One pastor said, "We just believed God, and He did the rest." That sounds beautiful, but it wasn't to me. I felt like God had forgotten us. I sat with tears streaming down my cheeks. I went and spoke to a seasoned pastor from the "just believed God" church. I asked him why God does not do for us what He has done for them. We believe God, but it just feels like we're climbing up a very steep mountain on a narrow path with a heavy load. It seems like we take two steps forward only to fall three steps backwards.

This wise man of God said to me, "Donna, there are seasons in ministry. This is the season you are in. In God's good time, He'll do great things."

We're nine years into this ministry, and I'm still struggling to stay here. I think there must be many churches easier to pastor than this one. The Lord spoke to me shortly after this conversation. He said, "Donna, what will it take to make you want to stay?" I told Him, "I need a team of people to work with us. I would like a building where we can do ministry. That's it!"

Now I'll wait and see what God does. He is faithful. He doesn't speak to me like this often, but I'm feeling pretty forgotten by Him at the moment. Maybe that's why He spoke to me. If I lose heart with this ministry, that will be very bad. Bill needs me to want to be here.

I know God hasn't forgotten us. It just feels like it sometimes! It makes me think of the Bible story where the disciples were in the middle of the sea and the large waves were washing over the side of the boat. All the while, Jesus was napping at the back of the boat. I bet they would understand how I'm feeling.

The other day, Bill and I were driving out of town, and this song played on our CD player: "Little is much when God is in it..." The truth of that song deeply encouraged us.

> *It's unwise to compare the ministry you are in with others. The grass isn't always greener on the other side, even though it looks like it from where you stand. God's perspective is different. He insists that we keep our eyes on Him. We're required to build where we are in such a way as to please Him, knowing that our work will be judged (1 Corinthians 3:10–15). We must be faithful where we are.*

Today, when I was making supper, I was led to pray urgently for my two oldest children. Lisa is eleven and Martin is nine. They were taking the streetcar home from school for the first time. We had done it with them a few times. It's only one long streetcar ride to our home. I wasn't worried about them getting lost.

I began to pray, and finally it was time to meet them at the streetcar stop. The moment our daughter stepped off the streetcar, I could see that something bad had happened.

When we got home, she told me about a man who kept trying to rub himself very inappropriately against her. He would move wherever she would move. She should have pressed the emergency bar but was too intimidated. There were some high school girls watching and laughing the whole time.

I called the police, and they were at our house in ten minutes. I didn't expect them to come that fast.

A very kind policewoman sat and talked to Lisa. She asked for a description and exactly what happened. They asked her if she would be willing to ride the streetcar with them the next day at the same time in hopes she could identify him. She was hesitant to do that. They didn't push her. They told her if she's too shy to push the yellow strip, she shouldn't ride the streetcar.

I feel terrible that this happened. I hadn't anticipated anything like this, especially not the first time my two oldest made the trip themselves. Needless to say, we will be accompanying them for quite a while yet.

I'm thankful that the Holy Spirit alerted me to pray. I know this could have been much worse. People have said to me, "Don't you think it's dangerous raising your kids in the heart of the city?" It *is* dangerous, but the Lord is with us. He watches over our kids. While what happened today was bad, the Lord was with Lisa. We had a good time talking and praying with her this evening.

Missionaries go to dangerous places all over the world and take their kids. Is potential danger bad? Should we not go where our Lord sends us? Do we always have to be comfortable and safe?

We've had a nice summer break. We rented a cottage for a week and then took a trip to visit family in the States. We had a good time, except for one thing. Lisa has been very sick twice now, and I just don't think it's normal sickness. I took her to a doctor in the small town near where we were staying. He said she had the flu. I've seen the flu before—it's not like this. The doctor didn't agree with me. Regardless, I still think something isn't right with my daughter.

Lisa has been sick, really sick, for twelve hours straight. Every five minutes she vomits again. It may sound like I'm exaggerating the severity, but I'm not. We took her to a hospital nearby, and they treated us like we were bothering them. The doctors were also very unhelpful.

We're praying a lot. Bill spent the whole night on his knees beside her bed, though he did make a few trips to the bathroom. I also spent my night on the couch praying. I'm not good with vomit, but I do know how to pray. So that's what I did.

One week has passed, and Lisa is still sick. In fact, she continues to be sick all through the night. She's having cramps, and they're torture. Lisa was in so much pain she couldn't speak. She's twelve years old now.

That's it. I've had enough. We're taking her to Sick Kids Hospital. They will believe me when I say my daughter doesn't have the flu.

The pain of watching your child suffer is terrible. You wish with your entire being that you could take his or her place. My stomach is in a constant knot. I was thankful when Bill took her to the hospital. She was so sick that he carried her into the emergency room. I stayed home with the boys.

Now I'm sitting here praying. That's all I can do. Lord, be with my daughter.

They said Lisa has Crohn's disease. She's now on Prednisone. Sadly, this sickness runs in my family. My mom has the same disease, and my sister has its cousin, colitis. My mom was crying on the phone; she feels like she's responsible for Lisa being sick. I assured her that God knows what's happening.

Lisa is staying at the hospital and being fed through an intravenous tube. My mom, brother, and sister came to see her and brought supper for us. My sister has been here to visit every day. I'm so happy that she's willing to walk through this valley with us. I'll never forget her kindness.

I usually go home in the afternoon and make supper. Bill brings the boys over to the hospital after they finish school, and we have supper at the hospital.

A woman from another room in the hospital came to see us. Her son is also very sick with Crohn's. Her pastor has heard of us and suggested that she come to see us if she needed anything. Really? We have nothing to offer her. I couldn't believe any pastor would make such a suggestion. He clearly has never been through this before.

I heard the woman coming down the hall. She asked the nurse if I was around. Unfortunately, the nurse told the lady I was spotted in Lisa's room. I was exhausted, so I hid in the closet.

Some days, Lisa has enough strength to go to school in the morning. Her school is very close to Sick Kids Hospital. When Lisa goes to school, I wait for her to get back. This means that I'm alone in her room. These days, I have enough energy to care for Lisa and make meals for the family. While I'm sure that this woman is very nice, she's incredibly needy. Her neediness is understandable; she isn't certain that her child will live. This is a reality I understand all too well, considering Lisa's condition. I'm not sure if Lisa will make it through this sickness. She's losing more weight every day. Now she's down to eighty pounds. I feel guilty for not helping this woman. But, honestly, I know myself well enough to understand that I've very little strength to share.

The other night, Bill was walking down the street toward our home. A few of the dads from our street were chatting, and they stopped when Bill approached. They had somehow heard that our Lisa was extremely sick. They asked him how he was handling it. Before Bill could say one word in reply, one of the dads piped up and said, "We know—you're praying." Bill told them that prayer is the only way he knows to deal with such difficult times. It's amazing how closely people watch us live.

Lisa was allowed to come home for a few hours today. It's Halloween, and she wanted to hand out candy to the kids. She also wanted to bake cookies for the nurses. She seemed to really enjoy her evening. It must have been very hard for her to not be able to have one bite of the cookies she made. Lisa really is an amazing girl. Bill and I are struck by her prayers of thanksgiving for God's presence and His love for her. She prays for the nurses and those around her.

Bill and I were in prayer, and we both felt that Lisa needed to go for surgery immediately. We told the assigned doctor, but he disagreed. Despite his disagreement, we continued to pray. The next day we had a new doctor. We told her the same thing, and she agreed with us.

Lisa went to surgery. Following the procedure, the surgeon told us that it was a good thing Lisa went in that day. Her bowel had burst, and the poison from her intestine was leaking into her body. The surgeon said, "If the new doctor had followed the original plan laid out by the previous attending pediatrician, Lisa wouldn't have made it."

After allotted recovery time had passed, this nightmare was over. Lisa is regaining her strength and is putting on weight once more. My daughter made it! Praise God!

While I've been away caring for my daughter, God has done some amazing things in the church. It's very difficult to do ministry when you're going through such deep waters. I remember, however, that the work is His and not ours. Despite the difficult situation our family faced, the Lord continued His work in the lives of Toronto's downtown population.

Last night, we discovered something interesting. We had invited a homeless man to sleep at our house for a few nights. I forgot that there was a bottle of wine in our basement. It had long ago been given to us as a gift. He drank the whole thing. He also found some Lysol and ingested that. Then he left in the middle of the night. We had no idea, because we're so exhausted from everything that has happened with Lisa. We're just beginning to recover.

Around three in the morning we heard something downstairs. It was our guest. He was returning Bill's winter coat, which he had taken without our knowledge. He wasn't more than a kilometre from our house when God spoke to him in his stupor and said, "Bring that man's coat back." That's what he did. It's a good thing he returned Bill's coat. It's turning into a very cold winter, and that's Bill's only winter jacket. It's interesting that God will speak on our behalf even to a drunk man. The voice of the Lord can't be silenced.

Our church is moving into a rented building on Queen Street West. One of the elders was walking with Bill and me along Queen Street, and we saw a "for lease" sign. This was a shocking sight. It's very difficult to find an affordable rental property for a small church in downtown Toronto. We had been praying for a building and were trusting God to lead us. The rental property is on the second level, which means we have to climb twenty stairs to get to our floor. That's not a big deal to us, but it could be for others.

The building has a colourful history. It was previously used as a pornographic theatre and had recently become a tattoo shop. As you can imagine, the inside of the building isn't all that welcoming. First you have to go through an eight-foot-high black metal gate. Then you go up twenty stairs and through a heavy metal door. Once inside, the air seems heavy and dark, even when all the lights are on. It's a huge, empty space. There are tattoo designs plastered everywhere. It seems that the former renters attempted to stick them to every available surface. It was clear that the tattoos they made celebrated death and the underworld. The theme of darkness was everywhere.

We rented the space for a remarkably good price. We're going to meet with our congregation in a few days and ask the Lord to remove the darkness from the space so that His presence might fill it with light.

We've started construction. We have a lot of work to do, and God has brought us many people who are willing to work. Last night I even learned how to do some basic electrical work.

It was three months ago when God asked me what it would take to make me stay. Now we have a building and a staff of twelve wonderful people. We began partnerships with Urban Promise and with Child Evangelism Fellowship. With both of these partnerships came a wonderful team of new staff. We also have a new couple who have joined us full time. They're planning to go overseas, and we're supposed to help them get ready. They're apprentices—that's their title.

I've never thought of it before, but our work feels a lot like missions work. When missionaries come and visit, they often say the same thing. Toronto is a gathering place for all nationalities. When we go shopping for groceries, we encounter a wide variety of cultures. In fact, the diverse population is reflected by the products available on the shelves at the grocery store. We feel very privileged to be here. I need to learn how to do some ethnic cooking. Some of the groceries from these other cultures look really good!

God in His kindness sent a missionary couple home on furlough to be our friends. The Lord told me clearly, "They are My gift to you." And they have been.

Getting a space like 602 Queen Street West to look like a church won't be easy. Before we can even begin the construction of classrooms and a sanctuary, the city requires a very long list of permits. Each of them is tedious and expensive to obtain.

Something interesting happened today. We had to go down to the rental property below us and check the ceiling tiles. We needed to make sure they all had adequate fire safety ratings. Before we went exploring downstairs, many said that the tiles most likely were not acceptable. This would mean a lot more work and money on our part. However, once the explorers started flipping a few tiles, they discovered that they were in fact acceptable. We only need to replace about twenty in the back. That saves us thousands of dollars and a huge headache from the business below us. I'm not sure that they're happy about a church moving in upstairs.

The bills for the renovations are due any day. Our church has been doing a rotating fast for a few weeks now. We're looking to God to provide the $41,000 we need. These are expenses we were not anticipating. We're trusting Jesus for His provision. We have just enough money to pay for this month's rent, salaries, and ministry expenses. You know, the normal things. God has to help us and provide.

It's the last day of the fast. Bill called me through the day to report how the money was coming in. It basically all came in today, all but $3,000, which came in on Sunday. God just orchestrated it that way. He moved various people to give, mostly from outside our church. This is the signature of God, who is big enough to overcome anything and all in one day. Praise Jesus!

We're done the construction project at 602 Queen Street West and are ready to begin worship services! Everyone is excited. We've worked very hard to get this far, and the space looks really good. God provided the right people to do what was needed. We've spent so much time working on this place, we won't know what to do with our free time!

Our dedication Sunday was well attended. The worship singing was enthusiastic and heartfelt. God is so good.

Bill decided to start doing Saturday night services now that we have our own space. He wants to do it for people on the street and see if they will come. Last week was his first one. About ten people attended. Low numbers don't discourage Bill. He says that ten people is a start. He felt like Jesus was there in a beautiful way.

On the corner of Queen and Bathurst is a contingent of First Nations people. It's clear that life isn't easy for them. We would love to reach out to them, but we have no idea how. We're praying about it now.

There's a housing development very close to our church. We have a wonderful team of people who lead a "Kids Church" ministry every Saturday morning. It looks a lot like a vacation Bible school program, but it's not in our church. The program is in the heart of the community. Every week, the workers share Jesus with the children, and it's been beautiful to see the kids respond.

For several weeks now, we've had more children from the housing project attending our Sunday school than from our church families. This creates a few challenges for us as Sunday school teachers. We want to teach all the children lessons that challenge them. The truth is, some of them already love Jesus and know the Bible stories, while others have never heard them. We, the teachers, often meet near our kitchen in the back of our space before we begin our lessons and pray for the challenges we face. God, by His Spirit, always helps us to overcome the challenges.

I was thinking about a saying by C. T. Studd: "Some would like to live within the sound of church and chapel bell, but I would run a rescue shop within a yard of hell."

That's what our ministry feels like some days. The people from the street who make their way up the church's twenty stairs have very difficult lives. Their hearts are strewn with brokenness and ruin. They're out of solutions, and many times hope has eluded them for years. May God use His church to be a place where the old ways pass and the new ways come.

Two children who attend Sunday school have stolen my heart, an eight-year-old girl and her six-year-old little brother. They come from a particularly difficult home. Their mom is alone and struggles with a drug addiction. We've also been told that she's a dealer. The boy is especially difficult at times in class, but I love watching him as he hears about Jesus and God's love for him.

Last Sunday, I felt that I was supposed to pray for this little boy before he went into class. I asked him if he would mind. He was very happy to have me pray for him. So I did. I asked the Lord to quiet his young heart and give him peace.

Our children's pastor said to me later, "Whatever you did with that little boy worked. I've never seen him sit like that in class."

I did nothing but listen to the request of the Spirit of God. God, who is big enough, reached down into this young child's heart and brought peace to his troubled soul. That's what made the difference.

Psalm 34:18 says, "The LORD is near to the brokenhearted and saves the crushed in spirit." I love that there are no age limitations on this promise.

The Saturday night services are continuing. The attendance continues to be low. During the service, Bill meets all kinds of people. Every week is different.

Sometimes I go on Saturday to support Bill, but not very often. Usually I spend my time preparing for my Sunday school class. The kids are all at home, and I like to be around.

We have two teenagers now. It's a whole new ball game of parenting. I've told Lisa since she was tiny that she can date when she's thirty-one years old. She's sixteen now. She asked me the other day, "Mom, how old do I have to be to *actually* start dating?" I replied, "Seventeen." She thinks I'm so liberal now.

When Bill got home tonight, he had the coolest story to share with me. He was praying before the service, as he always does, and the Lord showed him something of a vision, of a woman with a very distinct mark on her face. The Lord was going to bring her to the service, and Bill was to pray for her. He had never seen this woman before.

As the service began, not one other soul was there. Slowly but surely, the people came straggling in. Then this very woman, with the distinct mark on her face, came into the sanctuary. Bill noticed her but continued with the service until it was finished. She showed no particular response, so he went up to her and asked if he could pray for her. She shared her story with him. She had recently been released from the Queen Street Mental Health Centre, just down the road from our church. Though she has always struggled with manic depression, she said that since coming out of the hospital she's had a different depression and wanted that lifted from her. Though she lives two blocks from the church, it had taken her all day to get there. She knew, though, that if she got there she would receive help. Bill prayed for her, and the depression lifted immediately.

I went to a district meeting today. A missionary doctor who works with women with AIDS was speaking. I was enjoying listening to her when in the middle of her great stories the Lord spoke very clearly to me. He told me that one day our son Martin will be a doctor overseas. I was suddenly in tears.

The thing is, Martin is in grade nine and has never talked about being a doctor. He wants to be a pastor. He also hates the sight of blood, which would be a bad thing for a doctor. I'll wait and see when God tells Martin this plan for his life.

We received a phone call from a woman who recently started to attend our church. She told Bill about another young woman who has been like a daughter to her. She asked if he could come and pray for her. She was in the hospital and very sick—near death, actually. She'd been in a coma for some time, with double pneumonia, collapsed lungs, a tracheotomy, and so on. She was in the intensive care unit with a poor prognosis. Bill said, "Sure," and off he went.

When he arrived at the hospital, he recognized the young First Nations woman whom he was asked to pray for. Brenda was at our intersection all the time, panhandling, often drunk. As she lay there in a coma, her life ebbing away, Bill anointed her with oil and prayed over her as the Scriptures teach us to do, asking for divine healing. Following his prayer, she remained completely unresponsive.

A few days later Bill was walking down Queen Street and there, panhandling again, was this same woman, quite healed, the hole in her throat sewn shut. Her face lit up like a Christmas tree when she saw Bill. Someone had told her that he had prayed for her. Brenda had a light that seemed to shine from her face. She came to faith in Christ very soon after that.

For the rest of that day, many of the First Nations people from the corner came up the twenty stairs, all of them for the first time, and introduced themselves to Bill, the man who prayed for their friend. They had all heard the story about Bill visiting Brenda in the hospital. As it turned out, she was related to many of them. It was very plain to all that God had done this in answer to prayer. They were very warm to Bill, and each thanked him for his prayers. That day, God opened the way for us into the hearts of the First Nations people of this community.

God is indeed our healer. He is alive and well!

Bill and a few of the men of our church have helped a woman move seven times now. She's exhausting. The district superintendent told us that the people who ask the most of us seldom stick around. We'll see. Hopefully this isn't the case.

A woman phoned the church today. She wanted the church to pay her dog's grooming bill. Bill kindly said no. I was glad it was Bill she spoke to. I'm not sure I would have been as gentle and loving in my reply. This woman often comes to the church. Her life is in disarray. Regardless, our well-frequented benevolent fund isn't for dog grooming.

Bill and I are going on a short-term missions assignment for two and a half weeks. Our two youngest will be taken care of by some of the great people from our church; the other two are old enough to take care of themselves.

Bill will be leading worship music, and I'll be doing poolside encouragement—my own created title—for missionaries from the Arabian Peninsula. I've never before been to the Arab world. It's a long plane ride! I'm looking forward to meeting the people, seeing the sights, and, most importantly, being warm. After all, it's the middle of winter here. I hope the kids will at least keep the house clean until we get back.

The Arab world is very different from Canada. Bill would love to move here and make this our new ministry. I like the weather and the people. I must say, though, I don't enjoy the culture at all. I told Bill, "If God wants us to come here, He'll have to write me a letter."

We're heading home tomorrow. It's been amazing to sit with these missionaries and hear their stories. We've thoroughly enjoyed being with all of them. They're brave people and faithful servants! I have the deepest respect for each one of them.

We received a huge but amazing gift when we returned home. I still can't believe it. Some of our staff picked us up from the airport, which was great. Bill and I were both very tired.

Once at the door, I noticed a few things. First, there was a huge sign in the window that read "Welcome Home Mom and Dad!" The sign was not in any of my kids' writing. Also, none of our kids would ever think to do something like that. Furthermore, Bill and I noticed a new doorbell. We both thought there was no way any of our children decided to replace the doorbell while we were away. We were mystified.

When we opened the door, there was a cameraman and a number of people from our congregation in our living room! Our children were also there. We noticed immediately that the living room was painted and decorated beautifully. In addition, there were new lights, new appliances in our kitchen, new carpeting up the stairs and down the hall, a new upstairs bathroom, an entirely redone upstairs, new decor in our bedroom, and new flooring where it was most needed. They even removed a wall and opened up the entranceway to the house. Bill and I were speechless!

It was an amazing gift. They did it all because of their love for us. We're forever thankful to all who laboured on this unexpected project. It's astounding to us that they did all this in two and a half weeks! Apparently people donated money toward this project. From what we can tell by looking around, it must have been quite a bit of money!

God is good. I wish you could see my house now. We've always wanted to do this type of renovation, but we lacked the essential resources: time and money. The Lord took care of it Himself through His wonderful people.

There's a young man who has a special dislike for Bill and me, to put it mildly. He's been working at turning two of our children against us. Someone very kindly told us and then spoke to our kids. We're extremely thankful. The kids listened and have stopped spending any time with him.

It's very hard to understand some people. May God give to us grace to forgive and move on.

It's been remarkable to see the strength the Lord is bringing to the church. Words can't express how thankful I am. We have wonderful Bible college graduates coming now. They don't like watching others work but rather join in. Bill and I are so very thankful for them. We also have a wonderful elders board, and we're grateful for them. God has brought some new musicians to us as well. It means a little less for Bill to do. We're excited to see what God will do with all these new and talented people. The Sunday school program is bursting with kids. Sunday mornings are no sombre event, that's for sure! They're vibrant and alive. We've received a lot of encouragement from numerous people.

A little while ago, our district superintendent asked if he could bring all the district superintendents from across Canada to meet in our space. Bill agreed, and the meeting was held during this past week.

It was a privilege to have all these district superintendents see our ministry. There's a beer store a few doors down from Toronto Alliance Church. These leaders were mistakenly given the beer store address as ours. Needless to say, it caused some confusion for a few moments!

We found out there's a brothel a few doors down from our church building. We had no idea. Our missionary apprentices are partnering with another organization that's beginning an outreach ministry to local sex workers. They're all from China. These women can't speak English, so our missionary apprentices run an ESL class for them. Often, they have a meal together before class begins. They've just begun to teach them about Jesus. Some days, it really does feel like we're ministering in the devil's lair.

Someone threw up all over our sandwich board downstairs. I'm so glad I didn't have to clean it up.

A fellow who has joined us is clearly unique. There's a saying "A bit of knowledge can be dangerous." As we were working through a Bible study one evening, he blurted out, "Is it not true, Pastor Bill, that God is the alfalfa and the omega?" Once Bill had adjusted his train of thought and was able to comprehend this man's statement, he replied, "Something like that, my friend."

Bill was on a prayer walk by himself a few days ago. The streets are lined with houses, and people were everywhere. Children were on their way to school, along with their parents. As he was walking down the street, in the distance he saw a woman approaching, and he knew immediately that there would be trouble with her. When she was about seventy-five metres away she pointed at Bill and began swearing at him. She cursed and blasphemed the Name of God at length. They continued to walk toward each other until they were beside each other. Bill just kept walking. She turned around and continued the loud tirade until Bill was again at a distance of about seventy-five metres. People on the street must have thought Bill did something very bad to this woman to elicit such a response from her. However, Bill had never seen her before. Things similar to this have happened to him in coffee shops as well. There's definitely the sense here that we're on a battleground.

Scripture reminds us that the battle we fight isn't against "flesh and blood, but against the rulers, against the authorities, against the cosmic powers over this present darkness, against the spiritual forces of evil in the heavenly places"(Ephesians 6:12). The battle is real. We have an enemy who is crafty and powerful. He works through discouragement to defeat us. In Christ we find victory. You need to know this and not be fearful of the surrounding darkness. Christ is greater than any evil scheme. The devil may be noisy at times, but he has no authority over us.

There was a time when I was terrified of anything to do with Satan and his demons. It wasn't until I came to the realization of who I am in Christ that I found freedom from this gripping fear. A godly man prayed for me on that day. Since then I have no fear of Satan, but I confess that he does make me mad.

I've been quite encouraged of late. Several Christians have visited our church for different reasons. The moment they walk into our building, even while they're making their way up the twenty stairs, they're overwhelmed by the contrast between the unrest of the streets and the peace that comes from God's presence in our place. Some were so moved, they began to tear up.

What does it mean to thrive in ministry? Not just to endure it, being faithful to a call, but to thrive in it? Paying careful attention to one's marriage is of great importance. When this is taken for granted, it comes back to face you. Marital difficulties impact everyone despite their vocation, ministry or otherwise. When both partners are supporting each other, it shows. If there's no support, it's visible. It's like both of them are walking around with a weight on their shoulders. Each partner needs to be in the other person's corner. In ministry, whether you are staff or an elder, you are on the front line of a battle. You need to be standing side-by-side with your spouse, eyes straight ahead. You need your strength for what is before you.

Where respect is lacking and love is being withheld, it's difficult to move forward. Strong marriages make for strong and effective warriors.

Then there's the sensitive issue no one likes to acknowledge or talk about much—mental illness. Because mental illness is such an uncomfortable and controversial topic, those who struggle with it often try their best to hide it from the world. Yet, after a while, people begin to take notice and heads begin to turn. When this finds its way into Christian leadership, it becomes particularly difficult—not necessarily impossible, just difficult.

So what does it mean to thrive in ministry? People come with great idealism into the urban core and have grand visions of bringing change to the brokenness of the city. They discover, however, that the city exposes fracture lines that are in their marriages and in their own souls, and if left unattended, they can bring great ruin on themselves. To care for your own soul and take time to nurture your marriage is of great importance.

Even though Bill and I don't struggle with mental illness, it doesn't mean we're ignorant of the subject. We've taken it upon ourselves to become educated in order to understand how to effectively deal with some sensitive situations that are the result of this type of illness. It's very challenging, to say the least. We try to be compassionate and understanding. As a pastor's wife, I often have to deal with my tired husband who comes home discouraged by what he sees day in and day out in the lives of individuals who face these challenges. We want to see people thriving and rising above the challenges that face all of them daily, not being crushed by them.

I've always found it difficult to know where to put my energy and time. There's no end of need or opportunity to serve Jesus. I love ministry and always have. I'm still a mother of four children. I can't neglect them. Hopefully I'm getting the right balance between ministry and family. I pray for the Holy Spirit's leading in my decisions. Before I commit to something, I talk it over with Bill. If he doesn't feel good about it, even if it's a wonderful opportunity I'll decline it. I have a tendency to over-commit myself. When this happens, I tend to get stressed out, and that affects everyone in my household. That's never good.

Our family has taken up canoe camping. It's wonderful! Bill and the kids are excellent canoeists. I'm pretty good at paddling, if I do say so myself. When the time comes for our yearly trip, we pack up and drive to the northern part of Algonquin Provincial Park, where there are few people. We usually see moose and listen to owls call. I love doing it as a family. We like it too that there's no cell reception and no worries from the city can track us there.

A few nights ago, there was a bear outside out tent. That was a bit alarming. He didn't hurt or bother us. But we could hear him breathing. He sounded very big.

Michael and Bill often go fishing during these canoe trips. Usually they can catch enough for our supper. One afternoon, they were heading back to our campsite and dragging the fish behind the canoe on a stringer, as is their custom. This time, however, a snapping turtle was following them—and it ate all the fish! When they realized all the fish were gone, they had to go back out and catch more. Only this time, they had to keep a sharp eye out for that snapper!

While we take a break from active ministry during the summer, Bill and I usually reflect on the year that has just passed. We know there's one area of ministry we need to improve on. We're very outreached-focused. I know our congregation must feel like we neglect them at times.

I see ministry like a boat on the ocean. In the water there are many lost souls, drowning. Some boats have very nice pools and spas available for the people aboard. Everyone seems happy and well looked after. However, the people aboard these luxurious vessels seldom go to the railing and look at the many people drowning below. Their lifeboats and ladders seldom go down, except for a few times a year.

Bill and I are often at the railing. If people want to talk to us, we ask them to meet us there, looking over at those in the water below. We need to be more balanced. It's something we're working on.

Taking a day each week as a Sabbath rest has been extremely life-giving. Though we lead very full lives, that day is different. On the Sabbath, which for us has been Monday, we withdraw from all ministry responsibilities and make it a day of rest. We protect this one day and look forward to it. Whatever the loose ends, they simply have to wait. A day of rest reminds us that we're not God and that the work is His. We know that we need a break, but even if we aren't tired, the Sabbath is still vital. God rested from His work, and He never gets tired.

There's more to be gained from the Sabbath than simply rest. It's on the Sabbath that we gain perspective. We find freedom from the addictive nature of our work. We have room to hear from God. We're free to take time to build into other important relationships. It was for good reasons that God said, "Remember the Sabbath day, to keep it holy" (Exodus 20:8).

One day, years ago, one of our sons was ten years old, and he voiced a concern to me. He was troubled about two homeless people who were staying with us for a few days. Bill and I knew they weren't the most pleasant people. We, however, felt that we were doing what the Lord had asked of us. In retrospect, the hospitality we showed these people was most likely foolish.

That night our son had a dream. The next morning, he came down to breakfast. He said that in his dream he was in heaven standing before God's throne. There the Lord spoke to him and said, "When you have done it to the least of these, you have done it to Me." Our boy then said to me, "Mommy, I may not like having these people here, but God does."

He was right. Helping people isn't always easy. "The least of these" are not always easy to reach out to. Generally, we prefer those who are similar to ourselves. As a result, we don't seek out those who are different. God's love is different than ours, isn't it?

A man, dressed very poorly, came up the twenty stairs to our church. John had shaggy grey hair with a bushy beard. He usually hung out in front of the church. He told us he had a room at the back of a house in the area. He was very nice and liked to come up just to have coffee. It was hard to understand him at times. He asked Bill for his business card, and not just one. He had enough to put in every pocket of every piece of clothing he owned. He was afraid that if he died, no one would give him a proper funeral. Many of his friends were from the streets, and some had passed away without anyone knowing. He didn't want that to be how his story ended.

One evening he came into the church, and it took everything he had to get up the stairs. He had cancer. When he finally caught his breath, he said he had no assurance at all that he belonged to God. Should he die, which was very probable, he didn't know if he would go to be with God—and this caused him extreme agitation that night. Bill shared a few Scriptures with him and then asked if he could pray for him. In the middle of the prayer, John suddenly stood up straight, like a young man with full strength. With conviction he declared to Bill, "I know now that I belong to God." And he walked out.

John died a couple of weeks later. God cares deeply for the souls of people who in the eyes of this world are largely invisible.

Today Bill came home discouraged. A fellow who has been a good friend sent him an email. He had no idea this man was unhappy in the church. He told Bill that he and his family won't be back. The church isn't growing fast enough for them.

What can I say to Bill to encourage him? God builds the church. If every person who ever came to our church had stayed, we would have a huge congregation.

Ministry feels like a dance at times. Two steps forward, a few more sideways, and then three steps back. I'm thankful that the church belongs to God. I'm reminded of Psalm 127:1: "Unless the LORD builds the house, those who build it labor in vain. Unless the LORD watches over the city, the watchman stays awake in vain." I often need to remind myself of this important truth. I also know that I need to forgive these people. God's people can be disappointing. May He give me the grace to forgive them. There's no point in becoming bitter. That would be very foolish of me. Besides, Jesus doesn't give me any other option but to forgive.

Last week we heard that my brother Doug had suffered cardiac arrest. He's one year younger than me. Bill and I have been in the hospital each day since. We brought our sons in to see him. He was in ICU, and the prognosis was very poor. Each boy went in one at a time and stayed with him, sometimes praying with him. Doug has tubes coming from everywhere in his body, it seems. As they prayed I watched tears slip down my brother's cheeks. His life is a very sad one. He's struggled with addictions since he was a boy. Our life growing up took its hardest toll on him.

When our son Martin, who is now in grade eleven, went in, I watched him through the room window. He prayed for Doug, talked some, and then stood there in silence. I knew something more was going on. When he came out he told me, "This just feels right to me. I think I'm supposed to be a doctor." It took two years for him to discover what God had already told me.

We got another urgent call from the hospital. Doug had been out of ICU for a few days, as they believed he was improving. But he suffered a second cardiac arrest. Bill and I went immediately to see him. He was lying on the hospital bed with the paddles to restart his heart right there beside him. His shirt was open. He was talking about nothing really, barely making sense. I stood by his bed and was rubbing his chest and praying for him silently. He asked me what I was doing. I told him, "I'm just rubbing your chest."

Doug said, "No, what are you doing?"

I told him then, "I'm praying for you, Doug."

He replied, "When you do that, all the voices inside stop."

Prayer is a mighty tool, and the Name of Christ is above all.

I was thinking today of how thankful I am for my kids. They see people as they are. They don't see the holes in their jackets or the messiness of their lives. This isn't because my children have had such great parents, though it would be nice if that were true. It has to do with the love of God that has flooded their hearts. I'm so thankful for the fruit I've seen in my children's' lives. God is love, and His love is for all people, no matter who they are.

I know that there may have been easier or nicer places for our kids to grow up, but I'm thankful He chose to put us here in downtown Toronto. The benefits far outweigh the costs.

I was thinking more about how God provides, not just for the church but also for my family. When our van broke down, we asked the kids what they thought we should do. With one voice they said, "Pray!" So we did. That very night the Lord put it on someone's heart to buy a van for us. He made some calls and gathered enough money to purchase a vehicle for us.

We had no idea this was going on. Later, he called to let us know that our van was waiting for us in a car lot out of town. That van has served our family very well over the years. Our children know beyond a shadow of a doubt that God is the One who provides for our family. I hope they will never forget this, as one day they will have their own homes and families. Hopefully our stories of God's provision will be passed down to their children.

My mother is very ill. I've been praying about her sickness for some time now. I don't think she'll recover. I've been spending a lot of time with her. It's heartbreaking to see her health failing. I went into her hospital room today, and she was crying. She found out that her brother-in-law has brain cancer and will not recover. My mother's tears were for her sister, who will have to endure the loss of a husband and a sister close together.

What sobering times. I have little energy for ministry in the church these days. I had to give up teaching Sunday school for several weeks. My heart is very heavy. The Lord gives me energy to make a meal for my family and to sit with my mother.

A pastor and his wife are visiting us at church for the week. They're very enthusiastic about almost everything. I confess, I don't have the energy these days for their enthusiasm either.

The visiting pastor's wife held a special function for the other wives. She shared with us about how to keep the sparkle in your sex life. Let me tell you, my head was nowhere near this subject area.

My mom passed away last night. I feel numb. It's been a long and sad three months. Some very kind people from our church came to be with us. Some of my other dear friends also came this morning and made me breakfast. I couldn't think straight. I can't remember a time when I was this tired.

The Lord is my strength, and it's in these dark times that I lean particularly hard into Him. He will sustain me each day.

Bill is rethinking the open invitation he gives to pray out loud during the concert of prayer event. In some settings it's relatively predictable who will speak up and what they'll pray for. One older woman who comes to this event is very sweet but a little simple-minded. Last week, Bill opened the floor to the congregation so that anyone might pray aloud. This sweet woman piped up with her honest and detailed prayer: "Dear God, please help my friend Rhonda Duberry, who is home with diarrhea. Help her to get better—always running to the bathroom like that." This week, she prayed, "Dear God, please help Woody. I had to kill him—he was so sick. I'm sorry, God. You know I had to do it." After the service, Bill and I had to explain to our visitors that Woody was her cat and she had to get the vet to put him down.

After a church service, Bill and I introduced ourselves to a family. We were kind to them, as we are to all newcomers. The wife gave me their phone number, as they have kids the same age as ours. I thought I would invite them over for dessert.

Later on, I called the number that was given to me. The husband answered. From what I remember, he was warm and friendly at church, but now he was very different. I invited them over for dessert, as his wife and I had previously discussed. In a harsh tone, he said that his wife was napping, and if they were interested in ever hearing from me again, they would call. He then hung up.

Wow! Maybe God rescued us from a potential nightmare. I feel sorry for his wife. I won't dare call again. This is another thing I need to give over to God. I'm thankful He's good at healing us when we come to Him.

Another woman who comes to our church is very ill. She suffers from a horrible disease. I don't know what it is exactly.

She loves to pray. She's first to pray at every prayer meeting. I feel very ungodly sometimes when I compare my own spiritual practices to hers, and it bugs me. Why does the Spirit of God always lead her first? Isn't there variety in these things?

Bill of course told me that her prayers are very precious to God. And, yes, he's right. Even still, it bugs me a bit. Although now I feel guilty admitting it.

I'm overwhelmed by the number of people we deal with who are struggling with addictions. These dear people have ruined their minds with alcohol and other substances. Some of them don't even drink beer—they drink Listerine. I'm never buying it again. My boys used to gargle with it for sore throats. I'm dumping it, and they can use warm salt water from now on.

I know that God is bigger than addictions. My heart breaks, though, for those we care for. They're up one day, sober for two, and then down for the count for several to follow. What a cycle!

One First Nations woman is a sister in Christ. She came in the other day and told Bill, "You have to help us, Pastor! We're looking to you. We're dying."

Bill and I are not powerful enough to save them, but we know One who is.

Our new Community Night ministry is continuing on Saturday evenings. We've learned a lot since we began. The supper that our partner churches provide is homemade and served by a combination of their team and ours. After this great meal we invite all our guests to stay for the chapel service. We also have a food bank and free clothing that we make available during the meal. And we have a wonderful parish nurse who does foot care and basic first aid. She listens to these dear people and prays for them. It's beautiful to watch her. Truly, it's Christ's love in action.

We're very thankful for the churches that partner with us, as the ministry is too much for us to do alone. We're grateful for the body of Christ.

We see a wide variety of people come regularly to Community Night. Many are from the streets. We see a lot of people who struggle with mental illness and are off their medications. There's no shortage of addictions as well. We meet people who are new to Canada and find themselves also in a place of need. It's a very mixed crowd. Each one who comes up the stairs has a unique story.

It's a challenge to see these people through the eyes of Christ. Some of them are very thankful, and others have an overbearing sense of entitlement.

Then we have to deal with stealing. We no longer have any clocks in our Sunday school rooms. They've been stolen. Our salt and pepper shakers go missing all the time. It's also a challenge keeping toilet paper in the dispensers and light bulbs in the sockets—they vanish regularly. Bill has to stop fistfights between people with anger problems. Sometimes people have had a bit too much to drink when they come up. For the number of people we serve during Community Night, our space is too small. It's not that there are too many people, but the group needs a lot of space.

One Saturday night, a gentleman I didn't know looked to be in rough shape. On the floor beside him was a yellow grocery bag that cockroaches were crawling out of. I have a special hatred for those creatures. I was sitting at that very table with some fellows I know well. None of them would kill the roaches. So I did! With my bare fist, I might add! It clearly demonstrated how deeply I dislike them. I was terrified they would get away. That's the last thing we need—a cockroach infestation. We already have to deal with mice. Bill and the staff have been at war with the mice for some time.

The Lord knows the heartache at those tables. He died for each person there and longs to be known by them. He wants this ministry to be about more than just feeding these people. He wants to heal them and set them free, replacing their despair with hope.

Jesus is in the business of restoring broken lives. This has become the mission statement of our church. It's what Christ does for each of us daily and what He longs to do in all of humanity.

I was deeply struck by a story Bill shared with me after one Community Night. A woman who regularly comes to this outreach asked if he would go to a bit of a memorial service in a cigar shop down the street and sing a song. The shopkeeper, just a young man, had committed suicide a few days earlier.

After the meal was served and it was time to leave the church, Bill, guitar in hand and with one of our elders at his side, headed over to the cigar shop. About twenty-five people from all walks of life were standing in a circle, heads bowed, quietly weeping. Bill knew intuitively that he was not to sing a song but to lead a memorial service. He put the guitar down, introduced himself, and asked if anyone had anything they wanted to share about this fellow, to remember his life. The first fellow read the suicide note. Then a few other people made some comments in response. Bill said it was beyond depressing. When it seemed right, he read a verse from a psalm. Right away, some people agreed strongly, putting their faith in God. Others, however, disagreed strongly, saying there was no way that could be true. Then Bill led out in the old hymn "Amazing Grace" and prayed for all who were present. Bill and the elder went around and shook the hands of those present, and then they left. It's remarkable how quickly the Word of God separates people.

We can't imagine or foresee the opportunities that come to share the Good News. The young woman who invited Bill was a prostitute. She's been working to get out of the lifestyle. She's found great comfort in Bill's teachings during Community Night. May the Lord Himself deliver her.

Bill phoned me today and said he would be late. Being late is nothing new for him—he often is. Today a man from the streets came up the stairs in tears. He asked Bill to talk with a woman in the back lane. She wanted to take her own life.

The back lane is littered with garbage and graffiti. When you look down the lane, it's common to see people sitting on the curb drinking. Bill found this woman sitting on a milk crate. He sat down beside her and listened to her heartache for a long time. Then he pulled out his Bible and read a few passages that he knew would bring her comfort and hope.

God was there and met that woman in the back lane. She left determined that God had a reason for her life and with a conviction that it was worth living.

I'm very thankful that we serve a Lord and Saviour who walks down the back lanes of this great city. He doesn't shy away from brokenness but rather is ready to step into it at a moment's invitation.

I've learned something very important over my years of ministry. The Scriptures tell us that the battle is the Lord's and not our own—not mine. The thought of the battle being mine exhausts me.

He's waiting for me every single day to encourage my heart and give me all that He's called me to.

I'm thankful that God never locks me out of the place of prayer. I need Him to fill me and give me hope every single day. The sorrows people face can be heartbreaking. I need a place to go and give these heavy burdens over to someone who is always present and more than able to care for them.

Last Sunday, a woman came to church whom I had never seen before. Neither will I forget her. She had green lipstick on. That was striking.

During the worship portion of the service, in the middle of one of the songs, I heard what sounded like several voices saying simultaneously, "We will not submit." It was this woman. Then she ran out of the church.

I hope we see her again. We know that Jesus can set her free.

Our oldest son, Martin, got his driver's license the other day. He was sitting in the living room boasting a little bit when the phone rang. Susan was calling to ask how his driving exam went. Without hesitation, Martin told her that he had passed. She said, "That's good, because I called every person in the church to pray for you." Susan may be a bit simple, but she's a woman of childlike faith. I know God hears her prayers. Instantly after hearing what Susan had to say, Martin turned red and thanked her for her faithful prayers.

Martin has been hoping to get into medical school when he's older. He told Susan that if he ever gets in he'll be sure to phone and thank her. He says it will be Susan's humble prayers that will open the door for him.

What a privilege it is for our children to know the love and prayer support of God's people in their own lives!

A psychic set up shop next door to the church about eight months ago. She moved out yesterday.

As we shared the same landlord, Bill asked him why the psychic moved. He said she directly blamed the church for ruining her business. She said her ability as a psychic was greatly hindered because the presence of our church was interfering. We're reminded that our battle is not against flesh and blood but against powers and principalities of this dark age. God is greater!

Last week all the district superintendents gathered here at Toronto Alliance Church. They had a two-day meeting in our building. On one of the days, Bill, who was taking care of their coffee breaks, realized he had no more cream. He quickly ran downstairs and to the nearest convenience store a few storefronts away. There he ran into a man who struggles with his sexual identity. He sees himself and identifies himself as a woman.

Bill knows him well. They've had many conversations, as he attends Community Night pretty faithfully. He works as a prostitute to support his addictions. When Bill ran into him outside of the store, he wanted to speak with him and wouldn't let him go. Somewhat anxious about the upcoming coffee break, Bill finally tore himself away and headed back into the church, cream in hand.

Unknown to him, the man from the street followed him up to the second floor. Bill was working at the back of the church, where the kitchen is, but when he walked back to the front with the tray of coffee and goodies, there the transgendered man was, visiting with all these godly men. They listened to him and made him feel like he truly mattered. What a blessing he was to them, and they to him. The men told Bill that the encounter really affected the tone of the meetings that afternoon.

God is very creative in the way He leads us to see His heart.

We had a wonderful encounter with the Lord this week. He reminded us that He is greater than the evil that seems to make itself at home on the streets of this city. Two of the women from the brothel two doors down from the church have come to know Jesus.

One woman, upon receiving Christ as her personal Saviour, felt a lingering darkness that she couldn't shake. A staff member who was working with her brought her to Bill for prayer.

The three of them sat in his office. Bill invited her to confess all her sins to God, and the staff member translated his words into her language. She looked at Bill in disbelief and said, "All of them?" That could take very long, she felt. She was fearful of even going down that painful path. She began, though, and was quickly taken over by weeping and deep sobbing. She laid sorrow upon sorrow before the feet of our Saviour. After perhaps ten minutes, she gradually quieted and became still. Then Bill took authority over the spirits that had been tormenting her. Immediately there was freedom, and she began to laugh. She had a difficult time opening her eyes, because the light in the room, she declared, was too bright for her. Everything seemed bright to her now that darkness was gone.

Soon after, she moved out of the brothel and found a new life for herself in another city.

After Community Night this week a young man came up our twenty stairs wearing only an empty cement bag around his hips. That was it! He wanted to know if he had to explain why he had no clothes or if we would be able to offer him something. We outfitted him without question or desire to hear the story. Some things are better left unsaid.

The generosity of poor people remains striking to me. Last week, one of the men who lives under the Gardener Expressway passed me a handful of nicely rolled dimes and nickels and asked if I could please put the money toward the fund for a new building, the one God has for us. God must have smiled.

Today our children's pastor and I took eight kids to another church to hear the story of Christ's resurrection. She's been teaching them about Jesus being our only Saviour. Some of the children are Tibetan. She told them that if they want to be one of God's children, they can't have the Dalai Lama *and* Jesus—it's one *or* the other.

She reminded them of this as we went to the very elaborate play. The Easter story was beautifully acted out. When it came to the part where the tomb was empty and it was clear that Jesus rose from the dead, all these children were so excited, they were jumping on the padded pews with sheer joy! When the invitation was given to receive Jesus as their Saviour, they ran as fast as they could to the front.

They came back glowing. Each one of them had chosen our Lord as their Saviour. What a day it's been!

Emergencies and ministry seem to walk together. As I think back over the years, I remember tragedies that happened, even in the middle of our holidays. Bill would drive back and forth to prepare for a heartbreaking funeral of a young man or woman.

Walking with people in their darkest valleys is something God calls us to. The people on the streets often consider Bill their pastor. He's conducted many funerals for street people.

Last week a man we knew came up to the church office. He had struggled for many years with alcoholism. It cost him his career and marriage. He longed to follow Jesus and give his life to God. He wanted to be done with his addiction to the bottle forever.

It was his fiftieth birthday that day, and he was desperate for a new start. He asked if Bill would pray with him. So Bill prayed as this man wept, kneeling low with his face to the ground before His Heavenly Father. It reminded us of the story of the publican who wept before God, beating his breast as he confessed what kind of a sinner he was.

He left at peace that Saturday evening, the light of Christ resting on him. He had a great weekend, sober. His friends told us he was better than they had ever seen him. He died on Monday morning of a heart attack. The Good Shepherd in His mercy called His beloved home.

One of the most disappointing things for us is when people we have helped outright lie about us.

On Saturday night a few weeks ago, there was a disagreement in the hall while people were waiting in line for the food bank. One of our workers settled the disagreement. As it turned out, the fight continued on the street below. Unknown to us, the woman at the centre of it all called 911 on the church phone. With one bulging bag of clothes we had given her and another bag full of food, she left and waited downstairs for the police to arrive.

Bill was beginning his message for the chapel service when several police officers came up the stairs. They were glaring at Bill. Bill wasn't sure what to do. It isn't easy to keep your thoughts in order when the police are waiting for you. In the middle of his message, Bill asked the main officer, "Can I help you?"

The officer replied, "I need to speak to you." Bill said he would be with him shortly.

He finished his message and went to talk to the officer. The officer was very upset with Bill and everything Toronto Alliance Church stands for. He told Bill what the lady who called 911 told him. Unknown to the officer, every word was a total lie.

The officer wouldn't hear Bill's point of view at all. Then he concluded by saying, "Your church, sir, is now a point of interest to the police. We will be watching you." He then turned around and left.

Bill came home feeling utterly exhausted. It was a hard night, and he had two more sermons to preach the next day.

"Now may our Lord Jesus Christ himself, and God our Father, who loved us and gave us eternal comfort and good hope through grace, comfort your hearts and establish them in every good work and word" (2 Thessalonians 2:16–17 NIV). Ministry needs to be

lived out in His strength, not our own. Ours runs out so quickly.
We need the Lord Himself to strengthen us and renew fresh vision
for us day by day if we're going to continue. It's much too hard for
us on our own.

Periodically I wonder, "Is it time for us to move on from this work?" Times of trouble abound. I know that's not a good basis for that decision. Seeming fruitlessness and things that never seem to change exacerbate those feelings—again, I know, a poor indicator. I know it's true that some plant, others water, but God makes things grow, in His time, His way.

I've also seen pastors leave a very effective ministry because of their spouse. They can become disheartened or discouraged. As a result, they begin to speak badly of the church or staff. It's bad news when a spouse speaks badly about another staff member or complains about the ministry to other members of the congregation. This is very damaging to a church, and I know it's not the way God calls us to resolve difficulties. Spouses who are unhappy can make it impossible to continue in ministry.

I find it very easy to run ahead of what God is asking us to do in ministry. There are a million great ministries going on. I hear about amazing programs people are running and immediately think we should try them. It reminds me of new diets and great ways to lose weight. I treat them the same way!

Yet God leads us all differently. I've discovered that it's a bad habit to continually compare what our church is doing to other churches. It's also not good to run ahead and start a program like the one a pastor friend is running just because it works for him. It's important to take our lead from the Holy Spirit. He knows what will work in our setting.

Listen to Jesus; don't ask Him to join your plans. Rather, find out
what His plans are and do that.

In light of the imperfections of people, mine and others, what does it really take to stay in ministry for the long haul? It's more than just being well-read in the latest ministry trends. The inner life must be strong in Jesus, and the spiritual house must be in order.

In addition, the discipline of prayer and fasting can be underrated in our Christian journey as ministers of the gospel. It always has a place. We desperately need to cultivate this discipline in our lives and experience with God.

There's a third thing that comes to my mind—tenacity and the discipline to live out of the strength and wisdom that only God gives. Without these qualities, one can't survive the battlefield of ministry.

One of the hardest things for me to deal with are the times when we fail people. It's hard to believe, though we work so hard and give so much of ourselves, that it's sometimes perceived as not enough—and maybe it isn't enough.

Some people believe that their issues are ours to solve, regardless of what difficulties we are facing personally. Then they leave the church, and we feel awful. I think, looking back, that this is the hardest thing we've had to deal with. It would be easier if they were to leave because their work took them away. The other scenario just breaks my heart. I've often thought, if I could just love the people less, it would be so much easier.

God asks us to love our congregation. We do love them, but we also fail sometimes. It's not always what we do that gets us into trouble but what we didn't do that they believe we should have. Right or wrong, we find ourselves in a position of asking forgiveness. The Scriptures teach, "If possible, so far as it depends on you, live peaceably with all" (Romans 12:18).

The journey with some people, as well as seeing fruit of our labours, can take a long time.

Ten years ago, a young woman came to our Tibetan teahouse, a ministry we ran for ten days while the Dalai Lama was visiting Toronto. We opened our doors for spiritual discussions and invited people to come and dialogue with us on the differences between Buddhism and Christianity. It was an exciting ten days. One of the young women who came was a Muslim, originally from Egypt. It was the first time she had heard about Jesus.

Since then, she's come to countless Saturday nights and listened to the sermons. Last week, she decided to follow Christ. It's taken ten years. May the roots of her newfound faith go down deep.

Our church body decided to welcome children from the neighbourhood. It seems children are often ignored. Over the years, as we've reached into a housing development near to the church, many of the children have joined our Sunday school. They're welcomed and acknowledged by many.

I was twelve years old the first time I went to church. I can't remember anything they taught me, but I remember this: they loved and accepted me. They made me feel like I mattered. I think Jesus would do it the same way. If they had ignored me and made me feel like I didn't matter, I'm not sure where I would be today. I'm very thankful to the people of that church who took time to say hello and ask me my name.

Years ago, our children's pastor started to reach out to two sisters. She and many others cared for these girls very deeply. Everyone knew them and welcomed them with open arms. They joined our youth groups and were part of our church for years, until Children's Aid removed them from their home because their mom was dealing drugs from their residence. They continued their walk with God and found a church in the town they were moved to. As far as I know, they walk with God today.

We need to welcome people, regardless of age, talk to them, and make sure they know they're truly important to us and to God.

Some lessons we learned when we were canoeing relate to life and ministry.

Bill and I and my brand new puppy named Mac went camping this past summer. We canoed to a great campsite about an hour down the lake on a secluded island. There was just us and the owls, moose, bears, wolves, and a lot of birds.

We needed some groceries, so we paddled down the lake to the main entrance of the park. We jumped in the car and drove to town to grab what we needed. Then the paddle back began.

The lake was very rough, and the wind was set against us, blowing hard. We had to cross the lake to get to where the water was calmer. That was quite a paddle. I'll never forget it. The waves were coming over the side of the canoe, and we had to paddle hard, steady, and smooth. Bill is an exceptional canoeist, and I can hold my own, but he's much better at it than I am. Mac sat as still as he could. I think he knew we were in a dangerous situation.

While we paddled, Bill was yelling words of encouragement over the wind and the waves. I didn't really hear them, as it took all my concentration to make sure I put my paddle in at the top of the wave and pulled hard. My muscles were burning, but I knew that I couldn't stop. I was praying, and I set my eyes across the lake on an outcropping of rocks that we needed to get to.

I started to think how this was very much like our marriage and ministry. Bill was steering at the back, as he's truly better at it. Yet he depended on my hard strokes to keep us afloat.

In all of this, our strength is in Jesus, not in simply the skills of each other. Christ is our anchor in storms and on calm days. Our eyes must be locked on the One who is our guide, our deliverer, and our sustainer.

When we made it to the other side, Bill and I discussed this whole thing. We had just lived out, in forty-five hard minutes, a picture of our marriage over the years. It was a frightening journey, and we proved once again that we're a strong team. We were very thankful.

In marriage and in ministry you need to be a strong team to survive. It takes love lived out as written in 1 Corinthians 13. Truly applied, that love takes the enabling of God's Spirit and our willingness to choose rightly every day. Forgiving, and the willingness to do so, are imperative.

Our home is getting quieter with each passing year as the kids leave for university. Life will never be the same for us. It's great to see them making wise decisions, but it's a quiet ride home when we bid them farewell at the airport or drive them with all their belongings to a university in another city. I'm thankful that Bill and I have each other.

I sat on my front steps and watched all the children on our street heading off to grade school. I see parents walking beside them all the way. How quickly the years passed.

I'm thankful that all four of our now adult children love God and are following His call in their lives. I'm thankful for the good relationships we all share. That's an extremely precious gift.

A Christian woman named Sheila comes to our Saturday night ministry. Sadly, Sheila suffers from cancer. She told me a beautiful story this past week. She had to go to have chemotherapy but had no money or way to get to her appointment. She prayed and asked God to make a way for her.

When she went to wait for the streetcar, she continued to pray. She looked down and saw under her foot a Metro pass that was good for the entire month. She picked it up and went to her appointment, rejoicing in the loving care of her Heavenly Father.

I'm frustrated with myself, as I get very tired of being surrounded by need. Sunday mornings are busy and demanding, but that's not what tires me.

It's the never-ending need of the street people. They like to come up at the end of the service, usually every Sunday.

I know I should be gracious as they take yet more of Bill's time. I know I sound very unloving—sometimes I am! Bill stands and listens to what is needed and does what he can to help them. Usually it's food or a token for the streetcar.

I felt very convicted today. A woman named Barbara needed something. I was impatient and tired of waiting for Bill yet again. I had taught Sunday school and had people coming for lunch—now it was time to go. Barbara is a prostitute who is trying to get cleaned up. She told me that Bill has been very helpful to her.

Bill got what she needed, and we climbed down the twenty stairs together. Barbara turned to me and said, "I hope you get a chance to rest—you seem tired." I wish I had greater patience. Bill's seems endless. Mine is not.

God is gracious and kind to me. I know He sees and understands me. I also know He forgives me when I fail to see things through His eyes. My selfish attitude seems to get in the way of what He's doing right in front of me.

Barbara has cleaned up and is no longer on the street. We've not seen her for a long time. She sends Bill emails about how she loves taking care of her kids and is going to church every Sunday.

I love sitting in my backyard and reading while listening to the birds call to each other. Our back-lane neighbour likes to invite all his buddies over to his garage to drink beer, and sometimes they smoke up. Often they start by 11 a.m. I have baked cookies for them to go with their beer drinking. I want to keep on his good side—so far, so good. I also hope to share with him the difference Jesus makes in my life. I'm praying for the right time.

The other day I baked some cookies for a meeting I was going to. I had parked on our yard. When you park in your yard, as many people downtown do, you have to drive into the back lane and then go back and close your gate.

On this day, there were five high school guys, likely skipping class, rap dancing in the back lane. I was hesitant to leave my car running while I closed the gate, as they looked pretty tough to me. I was afraid they might jump in and take our car (not that it's cool or anything prestigious to be seen in!).

So before I drove out I went back into the kitchen and grabbed a bunch more of the chocolate chip cookies I had just baked. I went to the back lane and interrupted the rap dance and offered these tough guys cookies. I assured them I was not poisoning them. They gladly received them.

They held my gate open for me while I drove my car out and then closed it. They promised they would watch my yard for me. Who knew that warm chocolate chip cookies could have such an effect?

There's a church that gives us gift bags of hand-knitted sweaters, blankets, and diapers, with a few outfits for babies. They're very generous gift bags. We're given the privilege of handing them out as opportunity arises.

One time in particular stands out. I was walking down Queen Street right by our church when a woman named Rhonda said hello to me. I greeted her, and she told me about her son, who just had a baby with his girlfriend. She said he was in the Barn Restaurant, right by the church. It's a greasy spoon where many of the poor of our community will eat when they can afford it.

I asked her if the baby was a boy or a girl. She said a boy, so I raced back up our stairs to the church and grabbed one of the bags from the wonderful ladies at that church.

I showed Rhonda, and we went to give it to her son. He was a big guy who looked pretty tough. I wouldn't be surprised if he was part of a local gang, as he sure dressed the part. He was on his cellphone, looking down.

When his mom introduced me, he barely looked up from his phone. I placed this very large gift bag in front of him, and he looked up briefly and said thanks and then was back on his phone.

I asked him to please open it. So he took a look and started by taking out the hand-knitted sweater and then the matching hat and booties. Then he took out the hand-knitted blanket and put his phone down. He took out each beautiful gift in that bag and then thanked me sincerely.

I told him about the wonderful ladies who made all these gifts for his baby, and he was deeply moved. I told him, "Your boy matters to God, and his life is important. That's why these dear women took the time to make these gifts for your boy."

What a wonderful privilege to give these gifts to this young man! I could feel Jesus smiling as I left the restaurant.

Bill has been riding his bike to work these days. He loves it, and it's a very fast way to get to work. But drivers can be very careless around bikers, though our city is full of them. Today, a car hit Bill. He's okay. His hip is sore, and his face is scraped up. I don't think his bike will ever be the same.

Community Night was rough this week; I guess it often is. One of the men was drunk and fell asleep in a corner in the sanctuary. This isn't the first time. It was the end of the evening, and we were cleaning our twenty stairs. Bill woke the fellow up. He made it to the stairs, which were half washed by then. He coughed once, and then the throwing up started. I think he hit every stair. I don't actually know, as I ran to get Bill and asked that he or the other pastor please clean the stairs. My friend and I don't clean throw-up. What a way to end an evening!

One very cool spring day, our children's pastor, another staff member, and I were praying through a downtown park. In just a few weeks we would have our summer fun fair there for the children of the neighbourhood.

This is a small park just off one of the busy streets in our ministry area. We were seeking the Lord's blessings for the fun fair. We would be sharing the gospel with many children who had never heard of Jesus before. We took a while, walking the circumference of the park and praying.

As we were leaving, something behind me caught my eye. I saw a host of angels formed by a collection of glittering gold dust. It was like they forgot to disappear fast enough.

What a beautiful picture! We were deeply encouraged.

There have been seasons of ministry that have been very difficult. It's in those times that we hang on to two truths especially: God is Sovereign, and He has called us to this place.

It will not always be easy. People will leave us, and we will not always understand. We know that we need to trust Him with details that are not at all clear to us and may never be this side of heaven.

I thank the Lord for the way He gives spiritual gifts to us as needed. Bill and I have far more gifts in our toolbox than when we started this journey. He gives to us exactly what we need.

We're certainly not the whole Body! He equips all of us so we can serve Him well. Many people say it's important to serve where you are gifted. In a mature work, that's true. In a new work, I think it's different.

We've all had to serve in areas that were not our gift, but the Lord met us there and enabled us. The day came when someone who was gifted in that area came along, and we were then able to pass that work to them and serve where our gifts are stronger.

There are times in the service of the King where we simply do what is needed.

I was thinking today about a man we've known for years. He's well known by everyone in our church. Mark was trained as a master carpenter but was injured and lost an eye and could no longer work in the field he loved. He's developed a very serious drinking problem. Mark is a man who longs to walk with God sober every day, but the alcohol, which he calls his "medicine," has a very loud, booming voice in his life.

Bill came home from church one day and told me that Mark yelled down Queen Street, which was packed with people from all walks of life, "Pastor Bill! You give us hope!" Amidst all the grief and heartache of these people who have made their way up our twenty stairs, God often uses these same dear people to bless us. We serve the Good Shepherd, who gives hope to all who call upon His Name.

I'll never forget a conversation I overheard when I was taking a few seminary courses. Two young men who were heading into full-time ministry were discussing the salary and allowances they would each be requiring of the churches that would have the "privilege" (my words) of hiring them. They also discussed the hours they were planning to work: 9 a.m. to 5 p.m.

I found this conversation very sad. I don't know where they picked up this attitude, but I knew I would never hire them, regardless of how incredibly gifted they were. Ministry is something we do for God. It's not where we get rich and are entitled to make demands. We come as those who are called to serve God Himself. It's not a job. If you regarded it as such, you're in the wrong position.

God does take care of us. He does provide and make a way for us. We need to serve with the right motives or it shows very quickly. We need to be balanced in ministry, but there will be sacrifices. People die in the middle of the night. Other crises come at inconvenient times, and they're intense. You don't sign off because the five o'clock bell rang. We serve God, and that's our first calling.

I'm not saying life should not have some fun in it, but we're not nine-to-five people many days. There needs to be time to laugh and enjoy family and friends, certainly. And sometimes significant sacrifices will be required of us.

At Christmas, our church divides up about ninety donated frozen turkeys to distribute to people who would appreciate them. One evening Bill went to the apartment of an old woman who is here alone from the Ukraine. She was so pleased to see him. In her apartment was a table and a chair and a mattress on the floor that served as her bed. Bill brought her a handmade lap blanket some wonderful grandma from another church had made for us to give away. He also brought her a turkey and some groceries to go along with it.

She was so thankful. It's hard to imagine what her life must be like. She comes every Saturday night faithfully.

Bill went from there to a couple's apartment not too far away—quite a different story there. Bill had not seen the gentleman for quite some time. There he stood on crutches. He told Bill what had happened. He had been sitting in the bathtub having a bath when suddenly the floor gave way and he fell—tub, water, and all—into the apartment below! He broke his leg in the process and was in the hospital for a quite a while recovering.

Bill could say with all honesty that he had never heard anything like this before. He had a nice visit, prayed with them, and left them with their turkey.

The Scriptures tell us nothing is impossible with God. That's good, because so much that I see around me is beyond anything we can "fix." Only God can step in and do it.

A particular Saturday night was New Year's Eve, and a young couple, likely around thirty, was at church. They were missing a few teeth but were clean and very much at peace and happy. I stood right behind them in the line waiting to receive communion.

We were talking a little bit. They found out I was Pastor Bill's wife, and they told me that a year before he had prayed with them to receive Jesus as their Saviour. Immediately all desire for alcohol and drugs left them. They said they had been clean for a whole year. This was the first time in their adult lives that they were celebrating New Year's completely sober.

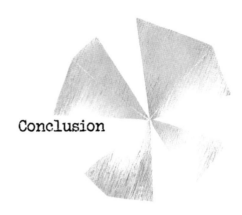

Conclusion

Ministry is like a dance with God, and He invites us to join Him in it. Some steps are harder than others, but He leads and we follow. It's always His dance, never ours.

We're all invited into this sacred dance, whether ministry is our vocation or not. God makes all kinds of unlikely choices in whom He calls into the dance—as He did with me.

May the power and the ministry of the Holy Spirit be upon you and fill you in every way.

Also by Donna Lea Dyck:

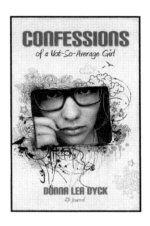

Confessions of a Not-So-Average Girl
9781770693364

I came from a messed-up home… really messed-up. When I was eight years old, beer bottles were flying and smashing against the wall downstairs… but then I found a brand new friend. I sat in my closet and wrote to him in my diary. *Confessions of a Not-So-Average Girl* is filled with raw and honest stories of how Jesus took an average girl with a shattered life and turned her into a Not-So-Average Girl by becoming her Saviour and best friend.

Learn more at
www.confessionsofanotsoaveragegirl.com

"Once you have read *Confessions*, you will want every child you teach to also read it, for Donna's story will help children who feel not-so-average feel like they are not-so-alone."

Melodie Bissell
—National Children's Facilitator of
The Christian and Missionary Alliance Church in Canada
President and Founder of Winning Kids Inc.